*This Faber Book of Bedtime Stories*
*belongs to*

_____

_____

The Faber Book of

# BEDTIME STORIES

First published in 2000
by Faber and Faber Limited
3 Queen Square London WC1N 3AU


Printed in Hong Kong
Designed by Sarah Hodder
Produced by Miles Kelly Publishing
Reproduction: DPI Colour

A CIP record for this book is available from the British Library

ISBN 0-571-19362-5
2 4 6 8 10 9 7 5 3 1

# The Faber Book of
# BEDTIME STORIES

*Chosen by Wendy Cope*

ff

# CONTENTS

We have given you an approximate time each story
will take to read aloud.

This book is for children and the adults who read to them. Sharing a story at the end of the day is a tradition that has, in many families, survived into the age of television and audiocassettes. It can be a perfect way to spend some quiet time together, something to look forward to, whatever else the day may bring. But it is unlikely to be a satisfying experience unless both parties genuinely enjoy the story.

A friend of mine used to read a translation of Homer's *Odyssey* to his children at bedtime. He swears that they loved it and I believe him. They loved it because their father loved it and enthusiasm is catching. In Anne Fine's *Goggle Eyes* the younger sister is spellbound when her mother's boyfriend reads her the financial pages of his newspaper. My choices are more conventional – all these stories were written for children but they have been selected with grown-ups in mind as well.

I hope both generations will be as captivated as I am by some of the characters – the iron pot crying "I skip, I skip" and scampering away on little legs; Aingelda Ardizzone's tiny doll in the freezer cabinet, playing with a plastic spoon and a pea; brave Teddy Robinson making the best of his night under the stars. I hope they'll laugh together at the drunken crocodile, in Leila Berg's story, as he dances out of the house and into the chrysanthemums, and at Penelope Lively's shiftless talking dog. I hope they'll be moved and inspired by Bombo, Ted Hughes's heroic elephant: "Though he is shy, he is the strongest, the cleverest, the kindest of the animals… we would make him our king, if we could get him to wear a crown".

I hold to the old-fashioned view that good books can have a good influence on their readers, especially when the readers are very young. Although none of these stories is heavily moralistic, I have paid attention to the values and attitudes they endorse. I was glad to find a charming and readable story (*Mrs Mallaby's Birthday*) about being kind to an old lady. *The Pedlar of Swaffham* is a wonderful, magic tale. That the hero gives most of his treasure to a good cause helped to clinch its place in this book.

Some of the stories I decided against seemed to me to equate physical beauty with goodness and its opposite with evil, or to suggest that there is no hope for a girl unless she is very beautiful, and that the sole aim of her existence is to get married. I like *Silly Simon* for its humour, and also for the relief I feel when Simon is rewarded with money rather than the hand of the princess. There is one story here about a good and beautiful girl who marries a prince: *Beauty and the Beast*. Adèle Geras tells the story so well that the reader, like the heroine, comes to love the beast as he is. When he changes into an ordinary handsome hero, we experience a moment of disappointment.

For a different reason I've avoided frightening stories. Many children love these, of course, and there is a place for them but not, I think, in a bedtime anthology. The monster in Terry Jones's story does, admittedly, come hunting for people to eat. And the heartless giant, in the tale that's named after him, also perpetrates some nasty deeds. I wouldn't classify either as really scary. However, if something scary is asked for, you could give them a try.

The timings on the contents pages are approximate and are bound to vary from reader to reader. I probably don't need to point out that, if you can't face reading for more than ten minutes, you could make the longer stories into serials.

My thanks for advice and suggestions to Adèle Geras, Mary Hinton, and Elizabeth Taylor (of Winchester, not Hollywood), to Paula Borton for her excellent work liasing with illustrators and to Suzy Jenvey of Faber and Faber, who talked me into editing this anthology and has helped to make it an entirely agreeable task.

*Wendy Cope*

# THE OLD IRON POT
*Anonymous*

ONCE there was a rich man who lived in a beautiful house. He was by far the richest man in all the countryside, but he was also a greedy master. The people who worked for him were very poor, because he paid them small wages for their hard work.

Not far from the rich man's house there was a lowly cottage in which lived a poor old farmer and his wife. They had worked for the rich man for many years, but they had been able to save very little.

One day the farmer's wife said to her husband, "All our money is gone. The time has come for us to sell the cow."

"Sell the cow?" exclaimed the old man, thinking he had not heard aright. "Why, what shall we do without milk?"

"I don't know," answered the good wife, "but we must have a little money to live. The old cow should bring – oh, perhaps a hundred pounds."

The old farmer's eyes brightened and he said, "I'll drive her to market tomorrow morning."

Early next morning, he started to market, leading the cow.

"Be sure you get a good sum for her," his wife called out after him.

"I'll do my best," he replied.

The old man had not gone far along the highway when he met an odd-looking little man who asked, "How much is your cow worth?"

"One hundred pounds, I think," answered the old man.

"I'll give you this pot for her," said the stranger, holding up a three-legged iron pot which he carried on his arm.

The old man looked very much surprised and said, "That old pot is worth nothing to me."

Then up spoke the iron pot, saying "Take me! Try me!"

When the old man heard the pot speak, he thought it surely must be a magic pot, so he agreed to the bargain and the exchange was made. But as the farmer returned to his cottage, he recalled his wife's parting words, "Be sure you get a good sum for her."

"I'd better take the pot to the barn," he thought.

So he took it to the barn and tied it in the stall. Then he went into the cottage.

"Did you sell the cow?" the old woman wanted to know.

The husband nodded his head. Then he said, "Come to the barn and see what I have got." He led the way, carrying a lantern, and his wife followed.

"Look in the stall," he said.

At first the old woman was very much puzzled, and when she saw nothing in the stall but an old iron pot, she grew angry and said, "Surely you did not trade our cow for *that*?"

Before the old man could answer, the iron pot spoke up and said:

*"Take me in and scour me bright;*
  *Hang me over the firelight."*

"You see – it's a magic pot," said the old man. "Let us do as it asks."

So they took the pot into the house and scoured it until it shone. The next morning the old woman hung it over the fire. Soon it became hot and cried out, "I skip, I skip!"

"Tell me where you skip," said the old woman.

> *"I skip, I skip, as fast as I can;*
> *I skip to the house of the very rich man."*

Before the old wife could answer, the iron pot had bounded off the fire and jumped through an open window. She burst into a hearty laugh when she saw the little legs scampering down the road.

Now the cook in the rich man's house was troubled. She had made a rich plum pudding for dinner, but when she had tied it up in the pudding bag she found it was too large to go into the pot.

"What shall I do?" she said. "There's not a pot in the kitchen large enough to hold the master's pudding."

At that moment, through the open window and down upon the table jumped the old iron pot.

"Try me," it cried out.

"Indeed I will!" said the cook, and she popped the pudding into the pot.

Then the pot cried out, "I skip, I skip, I skip!"

"Tell me where you skip," said the servant.

> *"I skip, I skip, as fast as I can;*
> *I skip to the house of the very poor man."*

Before the cook could catch her breath, the old pot was hopping along the road again.

The poor man's wife was wondering what she could get for dinner, when suddenly the iron pot jumped through the window and came to rest on the table.

"Well," she said, "I see that the old pot has brought us a fine plum pudding." Then she called her husband for the meal.

When the pudding was eaten, the wife scoured the pot and set it on the fire. In a little while she heard it cry out, "I skip, I skip, I skip!"

"Tell me where you skip," she said.

*"I skip, I skip, as fast as I can;*
*I skip to the house of the very rich man."*

Out of the window leaped the old iron pot. The little legs pattered down the highway and across a meadow to the rich man's barn, where several men were threshing wheat.

"What shall we put the grain in?" asked one of the men. "The sacks from the village have not yet come."

"Here is an old iron pot," said another.

The men began to fill the iron pot with the wheat, and soon the pot held all the wheat the men had threshed.

"I skip, I skip, I skip!" cried the pot.

"Tell me where you skip," said a man.

*"I skip, I skip, as fast as I can;*
*I skip to the house of the very poor man."*

And out of the barn door leaped the old iron pot. It skipped over the meadow and down the highway to the poor man's house. With a great bound it went through the window and stood in the middle of the kitchen where the old woman was working.

"Come and see what the old pot has brought us," the wife called to her husband.

"Why, it's full of fine wheat," said the old man. "Let's empty it."

"It will last us for a long time," the wife said, as they poured out bushels of the wheat.

The pot was scoured again as bright as silver and set on the fire. Then, some mornings later, as the old couple were eating breakfast, the pot again cried out, "I skip, I skip, I skip!"

"Where do you skip now?" they both asked, and the pot answered:

> "I skip, I skip, as fast as I can,
> To the counting-house of the very rich man."

With a great bound, the pot leaped out of the window and pattered down the highway to the rich man's house.

On just that morning, the rich man was in his counting-house, where he kept all of his money. The table where he sat was covered with gold and silver coins. Suddenly something leaped through the open window and bumped against the table. It was the old iron pot, of course.

"Why, here's a good strong pot," he said. "It will do very nicely to hold some of my gold and silver."

He was surprised to find how much the old pot held, for indeed, he was able to pack *all* of his coins in it!

"I skip, I skip, I skip!" cried the pot.

The rich man jumped to his feet in alarm. Away leaped the pot out of the window and down the highway. It carried the money to the house of the poor man, who was standing in the kitchen.

Now it was his turn to call his wife. "Come quickly and see what the old pot has brought us!" he shouted. "Shining gold and silver! It's enough to last us to the end of our days!"

"Ah," said his wife when she saw the bright coins, "what a bargain you struck when you traded the cow for this pot! Now it need never skip again."

But as soon as all of the money had been taken out of the pot, the old man and his wife again heard it cry out, "I skip, I skip, I skip!"

"And where do you skip now?" asked the old wife.

But this time the pot did not stop to answer. It leaped out of

the window and hurried down the highway. As it came down the road, the rich man's cook happened to see it, and promptly told her master about it.

The rich man ran as fast as he could to meet the pot. He threw his arms around it and cried, "I've caught you this time!"

But then the strangest thing happened. The handle of the iron pot wound itself around the rich man, tying him up!

"I skip, I skip, I skip!" the pot cried.

Then off it started, dragging the rich man down the road to the poor man's cottage. This time it did not stop. When it passed the kitchen, the farmer's wife called out of the window, "*Please* tell me where you skip!"

And the last words the pot spoke, as it carried off the greedy man, were:

*"I skip, I skip, as fast as I can;*
*To the far North Pole with the very rich man!"*

*illustrated by James Mayhew*

# The Emperor's New Clothes

### *by Hans Christian Andersen,*
### *translated by Naomi Lewis*

MANY years ago there lived an Emperor. He was so passionately fond of fine new clothes that he spent all his money and time on dressing up. He cared nothing for his army, nor for going to the theatre, nor for driving out in his carriage among the people – except as a chance for showing off his latest outfit. He had a different coat for every hour of the day; and at times when you'd be told of other monarchs, "He's holding a council," in *his* case the answer would be, "The Emperor is in his dressing-room."

Life was cheerful enough in the city where he lived. Strangers were always arriving, and one day a pair of shady characters turned up; they claimed to be weavers. But the cloth they wove (so they said) wasn't only exceptionally beautiful but had magical properties; even when made into clothes it was invisible to anyone who was either unfit for his job or particularly stupid. "Excellent!" thought the Emperor. "What a chance to discover which men in my kingdom aren't fit for the posts they hold – and which are the wise ones and the fools. Yes! that stuff must be woven and made into clothes at once!" And he gave the two rogues a large sum of money so that they could start.

So the rascally pair set up two looms and behaved as if they were working hard; but actually there was nothing on the machines at all. Before long they were demanding the finest silk and golden thread; these they crammed into their own pockets, and went on moving their arms at the empty looms until far into the night.

After a time, the Emperor thought, "I really *would* like to know how they are getting on." But when he recalled that no one who was stupid, or unfit for his work, could see the cloth, he felt rather awkward about going himself. It was not that he had any doubts about his own abilities, of course – yet he felt that it might be best to send someone else for a start. After all, everyone in the city knew the special powers of the cloth; everyone was longing to find out how foolish or incompetent his neighbours were.

"I know, I'll send my honest old minister to the weavers," he decided. "He's the right man, as sensible as can be; and no one can complain about the way he does his job."

So the good old minister went into the room where the two rogues were pretending to work at the looms. "Heaven help us!" he thought, and his eyes opened wider and wider. "I can't see anything." But he kept his thoughts to himself.

The two swindlers begged him to step closer; did he not agree that the patterns were beautiful? the colours delightful? And they waved their hands at the empty looms. But though the poor old minister peered and stared, he still could see nothing, for the simple reason that nothing was there to see.

"Heavens!" he thought. "Am I really stupid after all? That has never occurred to me – and it had better not occur to anyone else! Am I really unfit for my office? No – it will never do to say that I can't see any cloth."

"Well, don't you admire it?" said one of the false weavers, still moving his hands. "You haven't said a word!"

"Oh – it's charming, quite delightful," said the poor old minister, peering through his spectacles. "The pattern – the colours – yes, I must tell the Emperor that I find them truly remarkable."

"Well, that's very encouraging," said the two weavers, and they pointed out the details of the pattern and the different colours worked into it. The old minister listened carefully so that he could repeat it all to the Emperor. And this he did.

The two impostors now asked for a further supply of money, silk and golden thread; they had to have it, they said, to finish the cloth. But everything that they were given went straight into their own pockets; not a stitch appeared on the looms. Yet they went on busily moving their hands at the empty machines.

Presently the Emperor sent another honest official to see how the weaving was going on, and if the stuff would soon be ready. The same thing happened to him as to the minister; he looked and looked, but as there was nothing there but the empty looms, nothing was all he saw.

"Isn't it lovely material?" said the cheats. And they held out the imaginary stuff before him, pointing out the pattern which didn't exist.

"I don't believe that I'm stupid," thought the official. "I suppose I'm really not the right man for my job. Well, I should never have thought it! And nobody else had better think it, either." So he made admiring noises about the cloth he could not see, and told the men that he was particularly pleased with the colours and design. "Yes," he reported to the Emperor, "it's magnificent."

The news of the remarkable stuff was soon all round the town. And now the Emperor made up his mind to see it while it was still on the looms. So, with a number of carefully chosen attendants – among them the two honest officials who had already been there – he went to the weaving room, where the rogues were performing their antics as busily as ever.

"What splendid cloth!" said the old minister. "Observe the design, Your Majesty! Observe the colours!" said the worthy official. And they pointed to the empty looms, for they were sure that everyone else could see the material.

"This is terrible!" thought the Emperor. "I can't see a thing! Am I stupid? Am I unfit to be Emperor? That is too frightful to think of."

"Oh, it is charming, charming," he said aloud. "It has our highest approval." He nodded in a satisfied way towards the empty looms; on no account must he admit that he saw nothing there at all.

And the courtiers with him stared there too, each one with secret alarm at seeing not a single thread. But aloud they echoed the Emperor's words: "Charming, charming!" And they advised him to use the splendid cloth for the new set of royal robes he would wear for a great procession taking place in the near future. "It is magnificent, so unusual…" Yes, you could hear such words all around. And the Emperor gave each of the impostors a knightly decoration to hang in his buttonhole, and the title of Imperial Court Official of the Loom.

All through the night before the procession day, the rogues pretended to work, with sixteen candles around them. Everyone could see how busy they were, trying to get the Emperor's outfit finished in time. They pretended to take the stuff from the looms; they cut away in the air with big tailor's scissors; they stitched and stitched with needles that had no thread; and at last they announced: "The clothes are ready!"

The Emperor came with his noblest courtiers to look, and the two impostors held up their arms as if lifting something. "Here are the trousers," they said. "Here is the jacket, here is the cloak" – and so on. "They are as light as gossamer; you would think, from the feel, that you had nothing on at all – but that, of course, is the beauty of it."

"Yes, indeed," said all the attendants; but they could not see anything, for there was nothing there to see.

"If Your Imperial Majesty will graciously take off the clothes you are wearing, we shall have the honour of putting on the new ones here in front of the great mirror."

The Emperor took off his clothes, and the rogues pretended to hand him the new set, one item at a time. They then put their arms around his waist, and appeared to be fastening his train, the final touch.

The Emperor turned about and twisted before the glass.

"How elegant it looks! What a perfect fit!" the courtiers murmured. "What rich material! What splendid colours! Have you ever seen such magnificence?"

"Your Majesty," said the Chief Master of Ceremonies, "the canopy waits outside." The canopy was to be borne over his head in the procession.

"Well," said the Emperor, "I am ready. It really is an excellent fit, don't you think?" And he turned himself round again once more in front of the mirror, as if taking a final look. The courtiers who were to carry the train stooped, as if to lift something from the floor, then raised their hands before them. They were not going to let people think that they saw nothing there.

So the Emperor walked in stately procession under the splendid canopy; and everyone in the streets or at the windows exclaimed, "Doesn't the Emperor look magnificent! Those new clothes – aren't they marvellous! Just look at the train! The elegance of it!"

For nobody dared to admit that he couldn't see any clothes; this would have meant that he was a fool or no good at his job. None of the Emperor's gorgeous outfits had ever been so much admired.

Then a child's puzzled voice was clearly heard. "He's got nothing on!"

"These innocents! What ridiculous things they say," said the child's father. But the whisper passed through the crowd: "That child there says that the Emperor has nothing on; the Emperor has nothing on!"

And presently, everyone there was repeating, "He's got nothing on!" At last, it seemed to the Emperor too that they must be right. But he thought to himself, "I must not stop or it will spoil the procession." So he marched on even more proudly than before, and the courtiers continued to carry a train that was not there at all.

*illustrated by Jane Ray*

# BEAUTY AND THE BEAST

*French fairy tale,
retold by Adèle Geras*

A VERY long time ago, in a distant land, there lived a
merchant. His wife had been dead for many years, but he
had three daughters and the youngest was so lovely that everyone
who saw her wondered at her beauty. Her name was Belle, and
she was as good and kind a child as any man could wish for.
When a storm at sea sank all but one of the merchant's ships, the
family was left with very little money, and Belle was the only one
of the three sisters who never complained.

"We shall have to clean the house now," sighed the eldest.
"And cook as well, I daresay."

"No more pretty new clothes for us," moaned the second sister.
"And no maid to dress our hair each morning and prepare our
baths each night."

"We are young and strong," said Belle, "and we shall manage
perfectly well until Father's last ship comes to port."

"You are a silly goose," said the older girls. "Hoping when
there is so very little hope. The last ship probably went down with
all the rest, taking our wealth with it."

Spring turned to summer, and towards the end of summer
came news that the merchant's last ship had indeed been saved
and was now docked in the small harbour of a town not three
days' ride from his house.

"I shall set out at once," he said, "and return within the week.

Fortune has smiled on us at last, and I am in the mood to celebrate. What gifts shall I bring you, daughters, from the grand shops that I shall surely see on my journey?"

"Something that sparkles like a star," said the eldest. "A diamond, I think."

"Something that glows like a small moon," said the second daughter. "A pearl to hang around my neck."

Belle said nothing.

"And you, my little one," said the merchant. "What would delight your heart?"

"To see you safely back in this house after your travels would please me more than anything," said Belle. "But if I have to choose a gift, then what I should like is one red rose."

As soon as the merchant finished his business in the harbour, he set off for home. His saddle-bags were filled with gold coins, for he had sold everything that had been on board the last of his ships. Even after buying a diamond for one daughter and a pearl for another, there was plenty of money left.

"But," he said to himself, "there are no red roses anywhere in the town. I must look about me as I ride, and perhaps I shall see one growing wild."

The merchant made his way home, lost in daydreams of how he would spend his new-found wealth. Dusk fell and soon the poor man realized that he had strayed from the roadway and that his horse was making its way down a long avenue of black trees towards some lights that were shining in the distance.

"This must be a nobleman's country estate," said the merchant to himself. Through tall wrought-iron gates, he saw the finest mansion he had ever laid eyes on. There was a lamp burning at every window.

Having no one else to talk to, the merchant said to his horse, "The gentleman to whom all this belongs is at home, beyond a doubt, and a large party of guests with him, it would seem. Perhaps he will extend his hospitality to one who has strayed from his path. Come, my friend. I will dismount and we will walk together up this handsome drive."

The gates opened as the merchant touched them. When he reached the front door, he said to his horse, "Wait here for a moment, while I announce myself."

He stepped over the threshold, but there was no one there to greet him, and a thick white silence filled every corner of the vast hall.

"Is anyone here?" cried the merchant, and his own voice came back to him, echoing off the high walls.

He went outside again quickly and said to his horse, "Come, we will find the stable, my friend, for everyone in the house seems to have disappeared. Still, it is a beautiful place. Perhaps I shall find a maid in the kitchen who will give me a morsel of food and show me a bed where I may spend the night, for we shall never find our way back to the highway in the dark."

The stable was comfortable and clean, and the merchant fed his horse, and settled him in one of the empty stalls.

Then he returned to the house, thinking that by now someone would have appeared.

There was no one to be seen, but a delicious smell of food hung in the air. Yes, thought the merchant, that door, which was shut, is now open, and someone is serving a meal.

He walked into this new room and saw one place laid at a long table. He saw a flagon of wine and one glass, and many china plates bearing every sort of delicacy a person could desire.

"Is there anyone here to join me in this feast?" said the merchant to the embroidered creatures looking down at him from the tapestries on the walls, but there was no reply, so he sat down at the table and ate and drank his fill.

"I think," he said aloud, "that I have come to an enchanted dwelling, and I shall now take this candlestick and see what lies upstairs. Perhaps a kind fairy has made a bed ready for me, and a bath as well."

He went upstairs, and saw that there, too, the lamps had been lit, so that he had no need of his candle. He opened the first door on a long corridor and found himself in the most sumptuous of bedrooms. The sheets were made of silk, and soft towels had been laid out on the bed. He could see curls of steam drifting from an adjoining chamber, and as he pushed open the door, he discovered a bath, ready for him to step into.

"Whoever you are," said the merchant to the velvet curtains that had been drawn across the windows, "you are the most thoughtful of hosts. I can smell the lavender oil you have sprinkled in the bath… Maybe in the morning you will show yourself and I will be able to thank you properly."

The merchant bathed and went to bed and fell into a dreamless sleep. When he woke up, the curtains had been pulled back, the sun was shining, and a tray with his breakfast upon it had been placed on a small table near the window. A fine set of clothes had been prepared for him, and he put it on and marvelled at how well it fitted. At first he could not find his own travel-stained garments, but they had been washed and dried and pressed and lay folded beside his saddle-bags, which he had left beside the front door the previous night.

"I must go home," he thought to himself. "However pleasant this place may be, I must return to my children. I shall fetch my horse from the stable and set off at once."

The gardens of the mansion were a small paradise. Seeing them spread out before him reminded the merchant that he still had not found a red rose for Belle.

"In this garden," he thought, "there may still be red roses, even though autumn is nearly upon us. I shall pick just one, if I see some, and be gone."

Flowers still bloomed in the garden, but the merchant had to walk along many paths before he came to a bush covered with red roses, that had just blossomed. He chose the plumpest and smoothest; the most luscious and velvety of all the flowers he could see, and snapped it off the bush.

At that moment, an anguished roar filled the air and there, towering over him, was the most hideous creature the merchant had ever seen; a being from the worst of his nightmares; something that could not be human even though it stood upright and wore a man's clothes and spoke in a man's voice.

"Ungrateful wretch!" this Beast said. "All that I have done for you: fed you and clothed you and sheltered you… all that is not enough. No, you must steal a bud from my most precious rosebush. There is no punishment but death for such ingratitude."

The merchant began to weep.

"I did not mean it as theft," he said. "The owner of this place – you – I knew how kind you must be. I thought a rosebud was but a trifling thing after all the wonders you had lavished on me. It is a present for my youngest daughter.

I promised her a red rose before I set out on my journey, or I would never have touched anything that belonged to you. I beg you, spare my life."

"You must not judge by appearances," said the Beast. "I love my roses more than anything in the world, and a red rose is no trifling thing to me. Now you have plucked one for your child. I will spare your life, but only on this condition. One of your daughters must return with you in a month's time, and you must leave her here for ever. She must come of her own free will, and bear whatever fate awaits her in this place. If none of your children will make this sacrifice for you, then you yourself must return and be punished for your crime. Go now. I will wait for you and for whichever daughter may choose to accompany you."

When the merchant reached his home, he wept as he told the story of the enchanted mansion and of what he had promised the Beast. His two elder daughters glanced first at the jewelled necklaces he had brought them and then at one another, but not a word did they utter.

Belle smiled and said, "Dry your tears, Father. It was for the sake of my red rose that you ventured into the garden, so I shall go with you and with pleasure."

The cold came early that autumn. As Belle and her father made their way back to the Beast's mansion, snow began to fall, and by the time they reached the wrought-iron gates, it seemed as though white sheets had been spread over the whole landscape. The merchant's heart was like a stone in his breast, and Belle was trying to cheer him as they drew near the house.

"You must not worry about me, Father, for if you do, it will make me very unhappy. I know that my happiness is your dearest wish, so for my sake, let your spirits be high. I want to remember you smiling." Belle smiled at her father, as if to set him an example. She said, "This is a very handsome building, and from all that you told me about the Master of this place, he seems to be a kind and hospitable creature. I do not see anything so terrible in living here, if your life is to be spared as a consequence."

"You have not seen the Beast," said the merchant, shivering. "Oh, you will change your tune when you do, my dear."

The door opened at their touch, just as it had before.

"We have come," the merchant called out, "as I promised."

His words floated up towards the ceiling, but no one appeared.

"Come," said the merchant. "Let us go into the banqueting hall and eat, for we have had a long journey, and you must be hungry, my dear."

Two places had been set at the table. Belle and her father were eating with heavy hearts when the Beast came silently into the room. It was only when he spoke that Belle caught sight of him, hidden in the shadows by the door.

"Is this the daughter," said the Beast, "who comes here in your place?"

"Yes, I am," Belle answered for her father. "My name is Belle and I am happy to be in such a beautiful house, and happy to be of service to my father."

"You will not be so happy," said the Beast, "once you have looked upon my face. It will fill you with horror and haunt all your dreams."

For her father's sake, Belle knew she had to be brave. She said, "I have heard your voice, sir, and it is as low and sweet a voice as any man ever spoke with. Your face holds no terrors for me."

The Beast stepped out of the shadows by the door, and the light of all the lamps in the room fell on his face. Belle's hands flew to cover her eyes, to shield them from the hideous sight, and it was with great difficulty that at last she peeped between her fingers at the Beast.

"Now," he said, "are you as ready as you were a moment ago to spend your days with me?"

Belle was quiet for a full minute, then she said, "I will become used to looking at you, sir, and then I will not flinch as I did just now. You must forgive me for my cruelty. It was the unexpectedness of seeing you for the first time. I shall not hide my eyes again."

The Beast bowed. "You are as kind as you are beautiful. Everything I own, everything in this place is yours to do with as you will. I shall keep out of your sight, except for one hour in the evening, when I will come into the drawing-room for some conversation. For the present, I beg the two of you to enjoy this last night together, for tomorrow your father must leave and return home. I bid you both goodnight."

The next morning, after her father had gone, Belle wept for a long time. Then she dried her eyes and said to herself, "Crying will not help me, nor despair. I must strive to enjoy everything there is to enjoy, and find the courage to endure whatever I have to endure."

She decided to explore the mansion, and found that everything she looked at had been designed to please her. There were books in the library, a piano in the music room, paints and pencils for her amusement, a wardrobe full of the most beautiful clothes that anyone could wish for, and everywhere invisible hands that made all ready for her and smoothed her way.

Beside her bed, on a small table, there lay a looking-glass and a note which read:

*"Whatever you may wish to see*
*will in this glass reflected be."*

Belle picked up the little mirror and wished that she might see her family and know how they fared, but the images that appeared made her so homesick, that at once she put the glass away in a drawer and tried to forget all about it.

And so Belle passed her days pleasantly enough, and every evening as the clock struck nine, the Beast came and sat beside her in the drawing-room.

At first, Belle dreaded this time, and the sound of the Beast's footsteps on the marble floors made her tremble with fear. But when he sat down, his face was in shadow, and as they talked, Belle's fears melted away, and the hour passed too quickly. Soon, she began to long for the evening, and to wish that she might spend time with the Beast during the day.

One night, as the candles guttered and flickered, the Beast stood up to take his leave of her.

Belle whispered, "Stay a little longer, sir. It is very lonely and quiet without you, and this hour is so short."

The Beast sat down again, and said, "I will gladly stay for as long as you wish, but there is a question I must ask you and I shall ask this question every night and you must answer me honestly."

"I would never lie to you, sir," said Belle, "for you are the best and most generous of creatures."

"Then tell me, Belle, would you consent to marry me?"

"Oh, no, sir!" cried Belle, and her hands flew to her mouth and she shuddered in disgust. "No, I could never marry you. I am sorry to say this after all your kindness to me, but oh, no, do not ask such a thing of me, I implore you!"

The Beast turned away from the light.

"I apologize for causing you distress," he said, "but I must ask this question every night."

Time went by. Belle and the Beast spoke of everything: of dreams and songs and poems and flowers and wars and noble deeds and merriment. They spoke of wizards and dragons and magic and marvels, of clouds and mountains and distant empires. They discussed Kings and Emperors, architecture and farming, families and animals. The only subject they never mentioned was love.

And still, as he left her side, the Beast asked every night, "Will you marry me, Belle?" and Belle would say that she could not.

At first she said it in words, but gradually, uttering the syllables that hurt the Beast so much began to hurt her, too, and she found

herself unable to speak. After that, she simply shook
her head and her heart grew heavier and heavier.

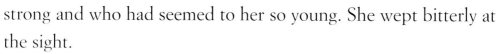

One night, after Belle had spent nearly a
year and a half in the Beast's house, she took
the enchanted mirror out of the drawer,
and asked to be shown her family at
home. What she saw was an old man
lying sick and feverish in his bed.
She could scarcely recognize her
dear father, who had been so tall and
strong and who had seemed to her so young. She wept bitterly at
the sight.

"I shall ask the Master to let me visit him," she decided. "He
would not refuse me such a favour."

That evening, Belle wept again as she told the Beast of her
father's illness.

"If you let me go to him, I promise to come back within the
week, only I cannot bear to see him suffering."

"And I cannot bear to see *you* suffering, my dear one. Take this
magic ring with you, and place it on your finger when you wish to
return to this place. All you have to do to be in your father's
house is look into the mirror and wish yourself transported."

"Thank you, thank you, dear sir," said Belle. "I shall be back
with you before you can miss me."

"And will you marry me, dearest Belle?"

"No, sir," said Belle. "You know I could never do that."

"Then goodnight," said the Beast, "and may you find whatever
it is you seek."

The next morning, Belle woke up in her father's house. His happiness at her return was so great that his health immediately improved, and even Belle's sisters were glad to see her. But every night at nine o'clock, Belle found her thoughts turning to the Beast, and she missed their conversations together and their shared laughter.

When the week was over, she was quite ready to leave, but her father's piteous tears persuaded her and she agreed to stay with her family for a few more days. "The Master will not mind," she said to herself, "for he is so kind and gentle."

On the third night of the second week, Belle dreamed of the rose garden. She saw in her dream the very bush from which her father had taken the red rose she had asked for, and under the bush lay the Master. His voice came to her from far away.

"I am dying, Belle," she heard. "Dying for love of you. I cannot live even one more day if you do not come back. You have broken your promise to me, and thus broken my heart…"

Belle awoke from the dream at once, cold and terrified.

Quickly, she put on the magic ring and lay back against the pillows.

"Take me back to him," she told the ring, and tears poured from her eyes. "What if I am too late and my Master is dead? Oh, let me be in time. Please let me be in time!"

Belle opened her eyes and she was once more in her bedroom in the mansion. Without even pausing to put slippers on her feet, she ran through the corridors and down the stairs and out of the front door. Breathless, she came to the rose garden, and there on

the ground lay the Beast, silent and unmoving. Belle flung herself
upon him and took him in her arms.

"Oh, Master, please, please do not die. I cannot, I cannot be
too late. How will I ever bear it if you die? Oh, can you not feel
my love for you? Come back to life and I will do anything… I will
marry you gladly, joyously – only speak to me, I beseech you."

Belle's tears fell on the Beast's hair as she kissed his eyes and
clasped him to her heart. At last he stirred and Belle looked down
at him for the first time. She found she was embracing a handsome
young man, and recoiled at once.

"You are not my beloved Master," she cried. "Where is he? I
love him. I want to marry him."

"Don't you recognize me?" asked the young man, who indeed
did speak with the Beast's own voice. "Don't you know me
without the mask of my ugliness? It is I, and you will never call
me Master again, but Husband and Friend. I am the same as I

ever was, and love you as much as I ever did. You have released me from a dreadful spell laid upon me in childhood by a wicked fairy who was envious of my wealth. She turned me into a monster until the day a woman would agree to marry me. Can you love me, Belle, as I really am?"

"I will love you," said Belle. "I *do* love you. I have loved you for a long time, though I did not realize it until last night. I love your face, whether it be beautiful or hideous, for it is your face and only an outer shell for your honourable soul."

"Then we shall be happy for ever," said the young man. "And the whole world will dance at our wedding."

Belle smiled and took his hand, and they entered their home together.

*illustrated by Pam Smy*

# THE RIDDLE-ME-REE
## *Alison Uttley*

"*In marble walls as white as milk,*
*Lined with a skin as soft as silk,*
*Within a fountain crystal clear,*
*A golden apple doth appear.*
*No doors there are to this strong-hold,*
*Yet thieves break in and steal the gold.*"

LITTLE Tim Rabbit asked this riddle when he came home from school one day. Mrs Rabbit stood with her paws on her hips, admiring her young son's cleverness.

"It's a fine piece of poetry," said she.

"It's a riddle," said Tim. "It's a riddle-me-ree. Do you know the answer, Mother?"

"No, Tim," Mrs Rabbit shook her head. "I'm not good at riddles. We'll ask your father when he comes home. I can hear him stamping his foot outside. He knows everything, does Father."

Mr Rabbit came bustling in. He flung down his bag of green food, mopped his forehead, and gave a deep sigh.

"There! I've collected enough for a family of elephants. I got lettuces, carrots, wild thyme, primrose leaves and tender shoots. I hope you'll make a good salad, Mother."

"Can you guess a riddle?" asked Tim.

"I hope so, my son. I used to be very good at riddles. What is a Welsh Rabbit? Cheese! Ha ha!"

"Say it again, Tim," urged Mrs Rabbit. "It's such a good piece of poetry, and all."

So Tim Rabbit stood up, put his hands behind his back, tilted his little nose and stared at the ceiling. Then in a high squeak he recited his new riddle:

"*In marble walls as white as milk,*
*Lined with a skin as soft as silk,*
*Within a fountain crystal clear,*
*A golden apple doth appear.*
*No doors there are to this strong-hold,*
*Yet thieves break in and steal the gold.*"

Father Rabbit scratched his head, and frowned.

"Marble walls," said he. "Hum! Ha! That's a palace. A golden apple. No doors. I can't guess it. Who asked it, Tim?"

"Old Jonathan asked us at school today. He said anyone who could guess it should have a prize. We can hunt and we can holler, we can ask and beg, but we must give him the answer by tomorrow."

"I'll have a good think, my son," said Mr Rabbit. "We mustn't be beaten by a riddle."

All over the common Father Rabbits were saying, "I'll have a good think," but not one father knew the answer, and all the small bunnies were trying to guess.

Tim Rabbit met Old Man Hedgehog down the lane. The old fellow was carrying a basket of crab-apples for his youngest daughter. On his head he wore a round hat made from a cabbage leaf. Old Man Hedgehog was rather deaf, and Tim had to shout.

"Old Man Hedgehog. Can you guess a riddle?" shouted Tim.

"Eh?" The Hedgehog put his hand up to his ear. "Eh?"

"A riddle!" cried Tim.

"Aye. I knows a riddle," said Old Hedgehog. He put down his basket and lighted his pipe. "Why does a Hedgehog cross a road? Eh? Why, for to get to t'other side." Old Hedgehog laughed wheezily.

"Do you know this one?" shouted Tim.

"Which one? Eh?"

"In marble walls as white as milk," said Tim, loudly.

"I could do with a drop of milk," said Hedgehog.

"Lined with a skin as soft as silk," shouted Tim.

"Nay, my skin isn't like silk. It's prickly, is a Hedgehog's skin," said the Old Hedgehog.

"Within a fountain crystal clear," yelled Tim.

"Yes. I knows it. Down the field. There's a spring of water, clear as crystal. Yes, that's it," cried Old Hedgehog, leaping about in excitement. "That's the answer, a spring."

"A golden apple doth appear," said Tim, doggedly.

"A gowd apple? Where? Where?" asked Old Hedgehog, grabbing Tim's arm.

"No doors there are to this strong-hold," said Tim, and now his voice was getting hoarse.

"No doors? How do you get in?" cried the Hedgehog.

"Yet thieves break in and steal the gold." Tim's throat was sore with shouting. He panted with relief.

"Thieves? That's the Fox again. Yes. That's the answer."

"No. It isn't the answer," said Tim, patiently.

"I can't guess a riddle like that. Too long. No sense in it," said Old Man Hedgehog at last. "I can't guess 'un. Now here's a riddle for you. It's my own, as one might say. My own!"

"What riddle is that?" asked Tim.

*"Needles and Pins, Needles and Pins,*
*When Hedgehog marries his trouble begins."*

"What's the answer? I give it up," said Tim.

"Why, Hedgehog. Needles and Pins, that's me." Old Man Hedgehog threw back his head and stamped his feet and roared with laughter, and little Tim laughed too. They laughed and they laughed.

"Needles and Pins. Darning needles and hair pins," said Old Hedgehog.

There was a rustle behind them, and they both sprang round, for Old Hedgehog could smell even if he was hard of hearing.

Out of the bushes poked a sharp nose, and a pair of bright eyes glinted through the leaves. A queer musky smell filled the air.

"I'll be moving on," said Old Man Hedgehog. "You'd best be getting along home too, Tim Rabbit. Your mother wants you. Good day. Good day."

Old Hedgehog trotted away, but the Fox stepped out and spoke in a polite kind of way.

"Excuse me," said he. "I heard merry laughter and I'm feeling rather blue. I should like a good laugh. What's the joke?"

"Old Man Hedgehog said he was needles and pins," stammered poor little Tim Rabbit, edging away.

"Yes. Darning needles and hair pins," said the Fox. "Why?"

"It was a riddle," said Tim.

"What about riddles?" asked the Fox.

*"Marble milk, skin silk
Fountain clear, apple appear.
No doors. Thieves gold,"*

Tim gabbled.

"Nonsense. Rubbish," said the Fox. "It isn't sense. I know a much better riddle."

"What is it, sir?" asked Tim, forgetting his fright.

"Who is the fine gentleman in the red jacket who leads the hunt?" asked the Fox, with his head aside.

"I can't guess at all," said Tim.

"A Fox. A Fox of course. He's the finest gentleman at the hunt." He laughed so much at his own riddle that little Tim Rabbit had time to escape down the lane and to get home to his mother.

"Well, has anyone guessed the riddle?" asked Mrs Rabbit.

"Not yet, Mother, but I'm getting on," said Tim.

Out he went again in the opposite direction, and he met the Mole.

"Can you guess a riddle, Mole?" he asked.

"Of course I can," answered the Mole. "Here it is:

> *A little black man in a hole,*
> *Pray tell me if he is a Mole,*
> *If he's dressed in black velvet,*
> *He's Moldy Warp Delvet,*
> *He's a Mole, up a pole, in a hole."*

"I didn't mean that riddle," said Tim.

"I haven't time for anybody else's riddles," said the Mole, and in a flurry of soil he disappeared into the earth.

"He never stopped to listen to my recitation," said Tim sadly.

He ran on, over the fields. There were Butterflies to hear his riddle, and Bumble-bees and Frogs, but they didn't know the answer. They all had funny little riddles of their own and nobody could help Tim Rabbit. So on he went across the wheatfield, right up to the farmyard, and he put his nose under the gate. That was as far as he dare go.

"Hallo, Tim Rabbit," said the Cock. "What do you want today?"

"Pray tell me the answer to a riddle," said Tim politely. "I've brought a pocketful of corn for a present. I gathered it in the cornfield on the way."

The Cock called the Hens to listen to Tim's riddle. They came in a crowd, clustering round the gate, chattering loudly. Tim Rabbit settled himself on a stone so that they could see him. He wasn't very big, and there were many of them, clucking and whispering and shuffling their feet and shaking their feathers.

"Silence!" cried the Cock. "Silence for Tim Rabbit."

The Hens stopped shuffling and lifted their heads to listen.
Once more Tim recited his poem, and once more here it is:

> *"In marble walls as white as milk,*
> *Lined with a skin as soft as silk,*
> *Within a fountain crystal clear,*
> *A golden apple doth appear.*
> *No doors there are to this strong-hold,*
> *Yet thieves break in and steal the gold."*

There was a silence for a moment as Tim finished, and then
such a rustle and murmur and tittering began, and the Hens put
their little beaks together, and chortled and fluttered their wings
and laughed in their sleeves.

"We know! We know!" they clucked.

"What is it?" asked Tim.

"An egg," they all shouted together, and their voices were so
shrill the farmer's wife came to the door to see
what was the matter.

So Tim threw the corn among them, and thanked them for their cleverness.

"And here's a white egg to take home with you, Tim," said the prettiest hen and she laid an egg at Tim's feet.

How joyfully Tim ran home with the answer to the riddle! How gleefully he put the egg on the table!

"Well, have you guessed it?" asked Mrs Rabbit.

"It's there! An egg," nodded Tim, and they all laughed and said: "Well, I never! Well, I never thought of that!"

And the prize from Old Jonathan, when Tim gave the answer? It was a little wooden egg, painted blue, and when Tim opened it, there lay a tiny carved hen with feathers of gold.

*illustrated by Kate Simpson*

# THE BEAST WITH A THOUSAND TEETH

## *Terry Jones*

ALONG time ago, in a land far away, the most terrible beast that ever lived roamed the countryside. It had four eyes, six legs and a thousand teeth. In the morning it would gobble up men as they went to work in the fields. In the afternoon it would break into lonely farms and eat up mothers and children as they sat down to lunch, and at night it would stalk the streets of the towns, looking for its supper.

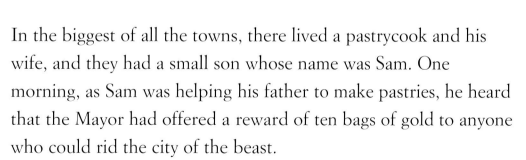

In the biggest of all the towns, there lived a pastrycook and his wife, and they had a small son whose name was Sam. One morning, as Sam was helping his father to make pastries, he heard that the Mayor had offered a reward of ten bags of gold to anyone who could rid the city of the beast.

"Oh," said Sam, "wouldn't I just like to win those ten bags of gold!"

"Nonsense!" said his father. "Put those pastries in the oven."

That afternoon, they heard that the King himself had offered a reward of a hundred bags of gold to anyone who could rid the kingdom of the beast.

"Oooh! Wouldn't I just like to win those hundred bags of gold," said Sam.

"You're too small," said his father. "Now run along and take those cakes to the Palace before it gets dark."

So Sam set off for the Palace with a tray of cakes balanced on his head. But he was so busy thinking of the hundred bags of gold that he lost his way, and soon it began to grow dark.

"Oh dear!" said Sam. "The beast will be coming soon to look for his supper. I'd better hurry home."

So he turned and started to hurry home as fast as he could. But he was utterly and completely lost, and he didn't know which way to turn. Soon it grew very dark. The streets were deserted, and everyone was safe inside, and had bolted and barred their doors for fear of the beast.

Poor Sam ran up this street and down the next, but he couldn't find the way home. Then suddenly – in the distance – he heard a sound like thunder, and he knew that the beast with a thousand teeth was approaching the city!

Sam ran up to the nearest house, and started to bang on the door.

"Let me in!" he cried. "I'm out in the streets, and the beast is approaching the city! Listen!" And he could hear the sound of the beast getting nearer and nearer. The ground shook and the windows rattled in their frames. But the people inside said no – if they opened the door, the beast might get in and eat them too.

So poor Sam ran up to the next house, and banged as hard as he could on their door, but the people told him to go away.

Then he heard a roar, and he heard the beast coming down the street, and he ran as hard as he could. But no matter how hard he ran, he could hear the beast getting nearer…and nearer… And he glanced over his shoulder – and there it was at the end of the street! Poor Sam in his fright dropped his tray, and hid under some steps. And the beast got nearer and nearer until it was right on top of him, and it bent down and its terrible jaws went SNACK! and it gobbled up the tray of cakes, and then it turned on Sam.

Sam plucked up all his courage and shouted as loud as he could: "Don't eat me, Beast! Wouldn't you rather have some more cakes?"

The beast stopped and looked at Sam, and then it looked back at the empty tray, and it said: "Well… they *were* very nice cakes… I liked the pink ones particularly. But there are no more left, so I'll just have to eat you…" And it reached under the steps where poor Sam was hiding, and pulled him out in its great horny claws.

"Oh… p-p-please!" cried Sam. "If you don't eat me, I'll make you some more. I'll make you lots of good things, for I'm the son of the best pastrycook in the land."

"Will you make more of those pink ones?" asked the beast.

"Oh yes! I'll make you as many pink ones as you can eat!" cried Sam.

"Very well," said the beast, and put poor Sam in his pocket, and carried him home to his lair.

The beast lived in a dark and dismal cave. The floor was littered with the bones of the people it had eaten, and the stone walls were marked with lines, where the beast used to sharpen its teeth. But Sam got to work right away, and started to bake as many cakes as he could for the beast. And when he ran out of flour or eggs or anything else, the beast would run back into town to get them, although it never paid for anything.

Sam cooked and baked, and he made scones and éclairs and meringues and sponge cakes and shortbread and doughnuts. But the beast looked at them and said, "You haven't made any pink ones!"

"Just a minute!" said Sam, and he took all the cakes and he covered every one of them in pink icing.

"There you are," said Sam, "they're *all* pink ones!"

"Great!" said the beast and ate the lot.

Well, the beast grew so fond of Sam's cakes that it shortly gave up eating people altogether, and it stayed at home in its cave eating and eating, and growing fatter and fatter. This went on for a whole year, until one morning Sam woke up to find the beast rolling around groaning and beating the floor of the cave. Of course you can guess what was the matter with it.

"Oh dear," said Sam, "I'm afraid it's all that pink icing that has given you toothache."

Well, the toothache got worse and worse and, because the beast had a thousand teeth, it was soon suffering from the worst toothache that anyone in the whole history of the world has ever suffered from. It lay on its side and held its head and roared in agony, until Sam began to feel quite sorry for it. The beast howled and howled with pain, until it could stand it no longer. "Please, Sam, help me!" it cried.

"Very well," said Sam. "Sit still and open your mouth."

So the beast sat very still and opened its mouth, while Sam got a pair of pliers and took out every single tooth in that beast's head.

Well, when the beast had lost all its thousand teeth, it couldn't eat people any more. So Sam took it home and went to the Mayor and claimed ten bags of gold as his reward. Then he went to the King and claimed the hundred bags of gold as his reward. Then he went back and lived with his father and mother once more, and the beast helped in the pastryshop, and took cakes to the Palace every day, and everyone forgot they had ever been afraid of the beast with a thousand teeth.

*illustrated by Ross Collins*

# A NECKLACE OF RAINDROPS

## *Joan Aiken*

A MAN called Mr Jones and his wife lived near the sea. One stormy night Mr Jones was in his garden when he saw the holly tree by his gate begin to toss and shake.

A voice cried, "Help me! I'm stuck in the tree! Help me, or the storm will go on all night."

Very surprised, Mr Jones walked down to the tree. In the middle of it was a tall man with a long grey cloak, and a long grey beard, and the brightest eyes you ever saw.

"Who are you?" Mr Jones said. "What are you doing in my holly tree?"

"I got stuck in it, can't you see? Help me out, or the storm will go on all night. I am the North Wind, and it is my job to blow the storm away."

So Mr Jones helped the North Wind out of the holly tree. The North Wind's hands were as cold as ice.

"Thank you," said the North Wind. "My cloak is torn, but never mind. You have helped me, so now I will do something for you."

"I don't need anything," Mr Jones said. "My wife and I have a baby girl, just born, and we are as happy as any two people in the world."

"In that case," said the North Wind, "I will be the baby's godfather. My birthday present to her will be this necklace of raindrops."

From under his grey cloak he pulled out a fine, fine silver chain. On the chain were three bright, shining drops.

"You must put it round the baby's neck," he said. "The raindrops will not wet her, and they will not come off. Every year, on her birthday, I will bring her another drop. When she has four drops she will stay dry, even if she goes out in the hardest rainstorm. And when she has five drops no thunder or lightning can harm her. And when she has six drops she will not be blown away, even by the strongest wind. And when she has seven raindrops she will be able to swim the deepest river. And when she has eight raindrops she will be able to swim the widest sea. And when she has nine raindrops she will be able to make the rain stop raining if she claps her hands. And when she has ten raindrops she will be able to make it start raining if she blows her nose."

"Stop, stop!" cried Mr Jones. "That is quite enough for one little girl!"

"I was going to stop anyway," said the North Wind. "Mind, she must never take the chain off, or it might bring bad luck. I must be off, now, to blow away the storm. I shall be back on her next birthday, with the fourth raindrop."

And he flew away up into the sky, pushing the clouds before him so that the moon and stars could shine out.

Mr Jones went into his house and put the chain with the three raindrops round the neck of the baby, who was called Laura.

A year soon went by, and when the North Wind came back to the little house by the sea, Laura was able to crawl about, and to play with her three bright, shining raindrops. But she never took the chain off.

When the North Wind had given Laura her fourth raindrop she could not get wet, even if she was out in the hardest rain. Her mother would put her out in the garden in her pram, and people passing on the road would say, "Look at that poor little baby, left out in all this rain. She will catch cold!"

But little Laura was quite dry, and quite happy, playing with the raindrops and waving to her godfather the North Wind as he flew over.

Next year he brought her her fifth raindrop. And the year after that, the sixth. And the year after that, the seventh. Now Laura could not be harmed by the worst storm, and if she fell into a pond or river she floated like a feather. And when she had eight raindrops she was able to swim across the widest sea – but as she was happy at home she had never tried.

And when she had nine raindrops Laura found that she could make the rain stop, by clapping her hands. So there were many, many sunny days by the sea. But Laura did not always clap her hands when it rained, for she loved to see the silver drops come sliding out of the sky.

Now it was time for Laura to go to school. You can guess how the other children loved her! They would call, "Laura, Laura, make it stop raining, please, so that we can go out to play."

And Laura always made the rain stop for them.

But there was a girl called Meg who said to herself, "It isn't fair. Why should Laura have that lovely necklace and be able to stop the rain? Why shouldn't I have it?"

So Meg went to the teacher and said, "Laura is wearing a necklace."

Then the teacher said to Laura, "You must take your necklace off in school, dear. That is the rule."

"But it will bring bad luck if I take it off," said Laura.

"Of course it will not bring bad luck. I will put it in a box for you and keep it safe till after school."

So the teacher put the necklace in a box.

But Meg saw where she put it. And when the children were out playing, and the teacher was having her dinner, Meg went quickly and took the necklace and put it in her pocket.

When the teacher found that the necklace was gone, she was very angry and sad.

"Who has taken Laura's necklace?" she asked.

But nobody answered.

Meg kept her hand tight in her pocket, holding the necklace.

And poor Laura cried all the way home. Her tears rolled down her cheeks like rain as she walked along by the sea.

"Oh," she cried, "what will happen when I tell my godfather that I have lost his present?"

A fish put his head out of the water and said, "Don't cry, Laura dear. You put me back in the sea when a wave threw me on the sand. I will help you find your necklace."

And a bird flew down and called, "Don't cry, Laura dear. You saved me when a storm blew me on to your roof and hurt my wing. I will help you find your necklace."

And a mouse popped his head out of a hole and said, "Don't cry, Laura dear. You saved me once when I fell in the river. I will help you find your necklace."

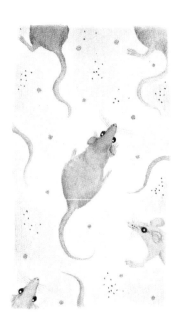

So Laura dried her eyes. "How will you help me?" she asked.

"I will look under the sea," said the fish. "And I will ask my brothers to help me."

"I will fly about and look in the fields and woods and roads," said the bird. "And I will ask all my brothers to help me."

"I will look in the houses," said the mouse. "And I will ask my brothers to look in every corner and closet of every room in the world."

So they set to work.

While Laura was talking to her three friends, what was Meg doing?

She put on the necklace and walked out in a rainstorm. But the rain made her very wet! And when she clapped her hands to stop it raining, the rain took no notice. It rained harder than ever.

The necklace would only work for its true owner.

So Meg was angry. But she still wore the necklace, until her father saw her with it on.

"Where did you get that necklace?" he asked.

"I found it in the road," Meg said. Which was not true!

"It is too good for a child," her father said. And he took it away from her. Meg and her father did not know that a little mouse could see them from a hole in the wall.

The mouse ran to tell his friends that the necklace was in Meg's house. And ten more mice came back with him to drag it away. But when they got there, the necklace was gone. Meg's father had sold it, for a great deal of money, to a silversmith. Two days later, a little mouse saw it in the silversmith's shop, and ran to tell his friends. But before the mice could come to take it, the silversmith had sold it to a trader who was buying fine and rare presents for the birthday of the Princess of Arabia.

Then a bird saw the necklace and flew to tell Laura.

"The necklace is on a ship, which is sailing across the sea to Arabia."

"We will follow the ship," said the fishes. "We will tell you which way it goes. Follow us!"

But Laura stood on the edge of the sea.

"How can I swim all that way without my necklace?" she cried.

"I will take you on my back," said a dolphin. "You have often thrown me good things to eat when I was hungry."

So the dolphin took her on his back, and the fishes went on in front, and the birds flew above, and after many days they came to Arabia.

"Now where is the necklace?" called the fishes to the birds.

"The King of Arabia has it. He is going to give it to the Princess for her birthday tomorrow."

"Tomorrow is my birthday too," said Laura. "Oh, what will my godfather say when he comes to give me my tenth raindrop and finds that I have not got the necklace?"

The birds led Laura into the King's garden. And she slept all night under a palm tree. The grass was all dry, and the flowers were all brown, because it was so hot and had not rained for a year.

Next morning the Princess came into the garden to open her presents. She had many lovely things: a flower that could sing, and a cage full of birds with green and silver feathers; a book that she could read for ever because it had no last page, and a cat who could play cat's cradle; a silver dress of spiderwebs and a gold dress of goldfish scales; a clock with a real cuckoo to tell the time, and a boat made out of a great pink shell. And among all the other presents was Laura's necklace.

When Laura saw the necklace she ran out from under the palm tree and cried, "Oh, please, that necklace is mine!"

The King of Arabia was angry. "Who is this girl?" he said. "Who let her into my garden? Take her away and drop her in the sea!"

But the Princess, who was small and pretty, said, "Wait a minute, Papa," and to Laura she said, "How do you know it is your necklace?"

"Because my godfather gave it to me! When I am wearing it I can go out in the rain without getting wet, no storm can harm me,

I can swim any river and any sea, and I can make the rain stop raining."

"But can you make it start to rain?" said the King.

"Not yet," said Laura. "Not till my godfather gives me the tenth raindrop."

"If you can make it rain you shall have the necklace," said the King. "For we badly need rain in this country."

But Laura was sad because she could not make it rain till she had her tenth raindrop.

Just then the North Wind came flying into the King's garden.

"There you are, god-daughter!" he said. "I have been looking all over the world for you, to give you your birthday present. Where is your necklace?"

"The Princess has it," said poor Laura.

Then the North Wind was angry. "You should not have taken it off!" he said. And he dropped the raindrop on to the dry grass, where it was lost. Then he flew away. Laura started to cry.

"Don't cry," said the kind little Princess. "You shall have the necklace back, for I can see it is yours." And she put the chain over Laura's head. As soon as she did so, one of Laura's tears ran down and hung on the necklace beside the nine raindrops, making ten. Laura started to smile, she dried her eyes and blew her nose. And, guess what! As soon as she blew her nose, the rain began falling! It rained and it rained, the trees all spread out their leaves, and the flowers stretched their petals, they were so happy to have a drink.

At last Laura clapped her hands to stop the rain.

The King of Arabia was very pleased. "That is the finest necklace I have ever seen," he said. "Will you come and stay with us every year, so that we have enough rain?" And Laura said she would do this.

Then they sent her home in the Princess's boat, made out of a pink shell. And the birds flew overhead, and the fishes swam in front.

"I am happy to have my necklace back," said Laura. "But I am even happier to have so many friends."

What happened to Meg? The mice told the North Wind that she had taken Laura's necklace. And he came and blew the roof off her house and let in the rain, so she was SOAKING WET!

*illustrated by Jane Ray*

# THE DISASTROUS DOG
## *Penelope Lively*

SOME people buy dogs. Some people are given dogs. Some people are taken over by dogs, as you might say. I'll tell you what happened to the Ropers, just in case *your* parents ever decide to get a dog from the local Animal Sanctuary.

Mr Roper was in favour of getting a dog from the Sanctuary because he didn't see the point of paying good money for something when you can get it free. Mrs Roper thought it would be nice to give a home to a poor unwanted dog. Paul, who was nine, didn't really care where the dog came from so long as they had one.

He'd been wanting a dog for ages, and now that they'd moved to a house down the end of a long lane, with no neighbours, outside the village, his father had come round to the idea. A guard dog, it was to be, a sensible efficient anti-burglar useful kind of dog.

The Animal Sanctuary seethed with dogs, in all shapes and sizes. They rushed around in wire-netting enclosures,

all barking at once, tail-wagging, jumping up and down. The Warden pointed out several promising creatures: a brown spaniel, all ears and paws, an elegant collie, a rather raffish mongrel with a penetrating bark. Mr and Mrs Roper moved along the fence, inspecting. Mrs Roper, who was a pushover for both animals and children, patted and cooed and allowed herself to be licked. Paul struck up a friendship with an over-excited yellow puppy.

"Oy...!" Paul looked around.

"Oy! You there..."

His parents were on the far side of the yard, discussing a terrier. The Warden had gone. The voice came from none of them. And I must explain that it was, and Paul immediately understood this, no ordinary voice. It was, as it were, a voice in the head – person to person, invisible, like a telephone. But the words that were said were ordinary and straightforward. Standard English. And so was the tone, which was distinctly bossy.

He looked at the dogs, carefully. They were all dashing around except for one, a nondescript brown animal with a stumpy tail and one white ear, which stood squarely beside the fence staring at Paul.

Paul glanced over at his parents; they were not looking in his direction. He stared back at the brown dog. "Did you say something?" he asked, feeling foolish.

"Too right I did," said the dog. "Do you live in a house or a flat?"

"A house. In the country."

"Central heating? Garden?"

"Yes. Listen, how come you…?"

The dog interrupted. "Sounds a reasonable billet. Get your parents over here and I'll do my stuff. Homeless dog act. Never fails."

"Can they all?" asked Paul, waving at the other dogs. "Talk?"

The dog spluttered contemptuously. "'Course not. Ordinary mob, that's all they are."

There was something not altogether attractive about the dog's personality, but Paul could not help being intrigued. "Then how did you learn?"

"Because I know what's what," snapped the dog.

"And why me? Why don't you talk to my dad?"

"Unfortunately," said the dog, "the adult of the species tends to have what you might call a closed mind. I've tried, believe you me. No go. It's only you small fry that are at all receptive. More's the pity. Go on – tell your mum and dad to come over and have a look at me."

Paul wasn't entirely pleased at being called small fry. He hesitated. The dog came closer to the fence and stared up at him, with slightly narrowed eyes. "Think about it," he said. "We could set up in the entertainment business. There'd be something in it for you – plenty of perks. The Dog That Can Count. The Dog That Can Read Your Thoughts. We could be on the telly. The sky's the limit."

"We just want a dog that can bark," said Paul.

The dog flung back his head and let out a volley of ear-splitting barks. "That do?"

Mr and Mrs Roper, abandoning the terrier, had come across. The dog immediately hurled himself at the wire fence with a devastating display of tail-wagging, grinning and licking. When Mrs Roper stooped to pat him he rolled over on his back with his eyes shut and squirmed in apparent ecstasy. Mrs Roper said, "Oh, isn't he sweet!" The dog, briefly, opened one eye. He then got up and squatted in front of Mr Roper in an attitude of abject obedience. Finally, he rushed off as though in pursuit of an unseen enemy and did some more barking, of hideous ferocity and quite deafening.

Well, I don't need to tell you what happened.

To say that the dog settled in is to put it mildly: he established himself. Within a matter of days. He got his basket moved from the cloakroom by feigning illness; Mrs Roper, gazing down at him, said anxiously, "I think perhaps he's cold in here. We'd better let him sleep in the kitchen by the boiler." The dog feebly wagged his tail and staggered to his feet. The first time they took him for a walk he developed a limp after the first mile. Paul examined his paws. He said, "I can't see anything wrong."

"Shut up," snarled the dog. "I'm crippled. I'm not one for all this hearty outdoor stuff, let's get that straight from the start."

Paul had to carry him home.

On the fourth day the dog said, "Tell her I don't like that rabbit-flavoured meat she's giving me. I want the beef and oxtail flavour. And more biscuits."

"Tell her yourself," said Paul sulkily. He was getting tired of being ordered about.

"Some people," snapped the dog, "might find things going a bit awkward, if they don't look out and act obliging. Some people might find for instance that their mother's best vase would get knocked off the table and broken and *then* who'd get the blame? Some people might find that things mysteriously disappeared, like their dad's pipe and people's gloves, and *then* who'd be nagged at to get down and find them?"

"You wouldn't!" said Paul, without conviction.

"Try me," said the dog.

"Why's she to believe I know what you like and what you don't like?"

"Children have a special relationship with animals," said the dog. "It's a well-known fact."

They called him Mick. It didn't seem to suit him particularly, but then it would have been hard to know what would. "What's your name?" Paul had asked, on the first day.

"Depends," said the dog. "One has run through a good many, as it happens. Suit yourselves."

So Mick it was.

His favourite activity was sleeping. Preferably after a hefty meal and on the best sofa or one of the beds. "Most dogs," said Paul, "rush about all day sniffing at things and asking to be taken for walks."

Mick yawned. "That's their problem. Me, I've learned how to keep my head down and have a comfortable life. Push off, there's a good boy, I want a kip."

To begin with, he barked at the postman and the milkman and the man who came to read the meter. On the fifth day, he slept through the window-cleaner and a man selling brushes and a lady collecting for the Red Cross. Paul said, "You're supposed to bark. That's what they got you for."

"I barked my head off all yesterday," said Mick sullenly. "Besides, there's a rate for the job. If they want more action, then what about something extra on the side? The odd chocolate biscuit. A nice chop."

Mr Roper, by now, was beginning to have doubts. He observed that Mick seemed a somewhat slothful sort of dog. Mrs Roper, always keen to see the best in people, wondered if perhaps he was a rather old dog and too much shouldn't be expected. Mick, looking worn, limped to his food bowl and stood there gazing at her soulfully.

Mr Roper said he was to be put out in the garden for part of every day, and no nonsense. Mick sat on the front doorstep, glowering. When visitors arrived for Sunday lunch he hurled himself at them, barking hysterically, and tore a strip out of Uncle Harry's trousers.

The smallest cousin burst into tears and refused to get out of the car and Mick was shut in the garage. When he was let out he was in a towering rage. "You're supposed to be able to tell the difference between friends and possible burglars," said Paul. "That was my uncle. Mum had to spend all afternoon apologizing."

"They said do guard dog stuff," snarled Mick, "so I did guard dog stuff. Anyway I didn't care for the fellow."

Other people, Paul realized, with resignation, have engaging roly-poly puppies; other people have dear old faithful sheepdogs; other people have sprightly interesting terriers. They had Mick. It was rather like having a very demanding guest in the house who is never going to leave. Only Paul, of course, knew exactly what sort of a person – dog – he was, but even his parents were beginning to be a little resentful.

"He is awfully greedy," said Mrs Roper. "I don't know how it's happened but he's somehow got me giving him *three* meals a day now." Paul knew only too well how it had happened. "He's lazy," said Mr Roper. "No two ways about it, I'm afraid." He took Mick for a five mile walk; Mick rolled in a muddy ditch and then came back and rolled on the sitting room carpet. "That'll teach 'em," he said. Paul, looking at his mother's face, realized with interest that Mick might go too far before long.

"I thought," he said, "we were going into the entertainment business. Do tricks. Go on the telly."

Mick, sprawled on the sofa, opened one eye. "Tricks? You must be joking, mate. That's work, that is. I know when I'm well off."

He got fatter and fatter. His attacks on the postman were more and more unconvincing. But the crunch came on the day the men came to collect the television for repair when everyone was out. They went round to the back door, which had been left unlocked, came in, removed the television and drove away in a van. Mrs Roper, when they brought it back, apologized. "I'm afraid our dog must have been a bit of a nuisance. I'd meant to lock him up before you came."

The television man laughed. "Not him. Fast asleep, he was, and then woke up and took one look and scarpered outside. Wouldn't say boo to a goose, he wouldn't."

That did it. "He's useless," said Mr Roper. Mrs Roper, always prepared to give the benefit of the doubt, suggested that perhaps Mick knew the difference between television repair men and burglars. "Not unless he could read the writing on the side of the van," said Mr Roper grimly. "He's going back to the Animal Sanctuary, and that's that."

Paul, secretly, heaved a sigh of relief. Mick had gone too far. And now, with any luck, they could get another dog: a speechless dog-like dog. What would happen to Mick he could not imagine, but he had a fairly strong feeling that he was well able to take care of himself. He said to him, "Why didn't you bite them? I mean, there they were, walking off with the telly…"

"I wasn't going to start mixing it with blokes like that," said Mick shortly. "I didn't like the look in their eye. Could have done me a nasty injury. I know when to keep a low profile, I do."

"They're going to take you back to the Animal Sanctuary."

Mick looked supercilious. "No skin off my nose. To tell the truth, I've known cushier billets than this. I'll tell you what I've got my eye on for next time – nice old lady. Soft touch, old ladies can be, I've tried 'em before. Plenty of nosh and no nonsense about exercise. I'll be all right – you see."

And something tells me that he was. But if ever you go to get a dog from an Animal Sanctuary, and happen to run across a brown mongrel with one white ear – well, I should think very carefully…

*illustrated by Wendy Smith*

# CLEVER CAKES
## *Michael Rosen*

ONCE there was a girl called Masha who lived with her granny at the edge of the woods.

One day Masha said, "Granny, can I play outside with my friends?"

"Yes, Masha," said Granny, "but don't wander off into the woods, will you? There are dangerous animals there that bite…"

Off went Masha to play with her friends. They played hide-and-seek. Masha went away to hide and she hid right deep in the woods. Then she waited for her friends to find her. She waited and waited but they never came. So Masha came out of her hiding-place and started to walk home. She walked this way, then that way, but very soon she knew she was lost.

"He-e-e-lp!" she shouted. "He-e-e-lp!"

But no one came.

Then very suddenly up came a massive muscly bear.

"Ah hah!" said the bear. "You come with me, little girl. I'm taking you home. I want you to cook my dinner, wash my trousers and scrub the floor in my house."

"I don't want to do that or anything like it, thank you very much," said Masha. "I want to go home."

"Oh no you don't," said the bear. "You're coming home with me." And he picked up Masha in his massive muscly paws and took her off to his house.

So now Masha had to cook and clean and wash and dust all day long. And she hated it. And she hated the massive muscly bear. So she made a plan.

She cooked some cakes, and then she said to the bear, "Mr Bear, do you think I could take some cakes to my granny?"

"I'm not falling for a stupid trick like that," thought the bear. "If I let her go to her granny's she'll never come back."

"No you can't," he said. "I'll take your cakes to her myself."

And he thought, "I'll eat all those cakes. Yum, yum, and yum again."

"Right," said Masha, "I'll put the cakes in this basket. Don't eat them on the way to Granny's, will you? Cos if you do, something terrible will happen to you."

"Of course I won't eat the cakes," said the bear.

As soon as the bear's back was turned, Masha jumped into the basket. When he turned round, he picked up the basket and walked off.

After a while, the bear got tired – ooh, that basket was so heavy, it was pulling off his arm – so he sat down.

"Now for the cakes," he said.

But Masha called out from inside the basket, "Don't you eat us, Mr Bear. We're little cakes for Masha's granny."

You should have seen that bear jump!

"The cakes heard me. Oh, yes, Masha did say if I ate them something terrible would happen to me. I'd better leave them alone."

So up got the bear and walked on… and on… and on… until he began to feel hungry. He thought, if I could eat the cakes without them knowing, surely nothing terrible will happen to me. But how can I eat them without them knowing? Then he said out loud, "Oooh, I wonder if those little cakes would like to hop out of the basket and come for a walk with me."

But Masha called out from inside the basket, "Don't you dare touch us, you great greedy glut. We're little cakes for Masha's granny."

The bear nearly jumped out of his jacket.

"Woo-hoo, those devilish little cakes knew that was a trick. What clever cakes. Next time I won't say anything at all. I'll just sit down and gobble them up. Yum, yum, and yum again."

So up he got and walked on… and on… and on…

But now the bear was getting really very, very hungry. It felt like there was a huge hole in his belly. This time he remembered not to speak. Very carefully he sat down, and slo-o-o-o-wly he reached out his massive muscly paw for the basket. But Masha, peeking through the holes in the basket, could see what the bear was up to and she called out, "Don't you dare touch us, you horrible great greedy glut. We're little cakes for Masha's granny and if you touch us, we'll jump out of the basket faster than you can blink, and we'll eat you up, ears and all."

"Zoo-wow, those cakes must be magic!" said the bear. "I'd be crazy to touch them. I'd better take them to Masha's granny as quickly as I can or something terrible will happen to me." And he hurried on to Granny's house.

When he got there he shouted, "Open the door, Granny!"

Granny came to the door and when she saw a great big bear standing there she was scared stiff.

But little Masha called out from the basket, "Look out, Bear, your time's up. Now we're going to eat you."

Bear dropped the basket, turned, and ran off shouting, "Help, help, the cakes are going to eat me, the cakes are going to eat me!"

As soon as the bear was off and away, out of the basket popped Masha. Oh, how pleased Granny was to see her, and how pleased Masha was to see her granny! They hugged and kissed each other so many times that there were no kisses left till the next day.

"What a clever girl you are, to trick that big bear," said Granny.

"Never mind that," said Masha. "Let's get these cakes inside us."

And that's what they did. Yum, yum, and yum again!

*illustrated by Brita Granström*

# A LULLABY FOR FREDDY
## *Adèle Geras*

WHEN Freddy the Fearless moved into the dolls' house there was great excitement.

"He's a soldier," said Keith, the little velvet frog. "I expect he'll have all kinds of stories to tell."

"He's bound to be tremendously brave," said Baby, the crocheted doll who never moved from the wooden cradle.

"And strong," said Minna the rag doll. "Have you seen how tall and straight he stands in his shiny blue and gold uniform? And isn't that a sword strapped round his waist?"

Freddy the Fearless turned out to be every bit as brave and strong as Baby and Minna had hoped. He was also very talkative, just as Keith had said he would be.

"I expect," he said, on the very first day, "that all of you are longing to hear tales of my soldiering… my bravery, assorted sagas of fights and battles and so on, aren't you? I mean, this is an extremely pleasant dolls' house, and they do say a change is as good as a rest, but it's not quite what I'm used to, oh no indeed!"

"Did you live in a barracks?" Minna wanted to know.

"In a fort," answered Freddy the Fearless, his voice full of pride. "A splendid cardboard fort in the middle of a sandy desert. There were palm trees and camels and we had battles in the morning. In the afternoon we marched around and had parades, and in the evening we all lined up on the floor of the fort for a spot of shut-eye. Oh, those were the days!"

"Where are all the other soldiers now?" Baby asked.

"Gone," said Freddy sadly. "Every last one. Dropped behind chests of drawers, exchanged for cars and things, taken away and given to the jumble sales if there was anything wrong with them at all, even the slightest scratch… oh, there have been so many casualties!"

"Well, we lead a very quiet life here," said Keith. "In the daytime, sometimes we are played with and sometimes we aren't."

"What do you do when you're not being played with?" Fearless Freddy wanted to know.

"We chat," said Baby. "There's always plenty to chat about."

"Oh, I'm just the chap you need then," said Freddy. "I know wonderful stories. I'll keep you amused for hours."

And he did. The first day simply flew past, and Minna, Keith and Baby heard about the Adventure of the Dining-room Table, and the Battle of the Desk, when Freddy rode on the back of a wooden elephant through tropical jungles of pencil trees.

Then there was the time when he fell into the Basin and bobbed about in the water for a full ten minutes before being rescued.

Then the night-time came, but it wasn't really dark in the dolls' house. There was a comforting triangle of golden light from the landing which shone into the room and into the windows of the dolls' house as well…

Keith rested his head on one of his pink velvet legs and prepared to dream of waterlilies. Baby stared at the pattern in the ceiling and wondered what she could pretend it was tonight. Minna flopped into the corner and listened to the night noises.

"That's a strange sound," she said to herself. "It's just like someone crying. But Baby doesn't cry, and neither does Keith, and everyone knows that brave soldiers never never cry. Who can it be?"

The snuffling went on and on, quite softly at first, and then louder and louder…

"Boo… hoo… boo… hoo."

"Is that you, Baby?" Minna whispered.

"No," Baby said.

"Is it you, Keith?"

"No," said Keith. "You woke me up. I was dreaming of waterlilies."

"Is it you, Fearless Freddy?"

"I'm afraid it is," came Freddy's voice out of the corner where he'd been put. "I'm sorry to say it is."

"But what's the matter?" asked Baby.

"I'm frightened."

"How can you be frightened?" Keith said. "There are no enemies here, and no battles. There isn't anything to be frightened of…"

"Yes, there is," said Freddy. "I'm frightened of the dark."

Minna, Baby and Keith thought about this for a moment.

"It isn't even properly dark," said Minna at last. "Look, there's a triangle of golden light shining through the door. Can you see?"

"But there are still dark corners," said Fearless Freddy. "And shadows. What's that, for instance? That big, square shadow just over there?"

"I expect it's my cradle," said Baby, "making a black patch on the wall."

"Isn't there anything we can do?" asked Keith. "What did you do in the fort?"

"Our general sang us a lullaby," said Freddy. "Only don't tell anyone I told you."

"And did that help you not to be scared of the dark?" Minna asked.

"Oh, yes," said Freddy. "It had special words, but I can't remember what they are. If only I could remember, I'd be all right, I know I would."

"I know lots of lullabies," said Minna. "I'll sing them and when you've heard them, you can tell me if I've sung the right one."

"Good show!" said Freddy, not sounding in the least bit scared. "Sing away!"

So Minna sang Freddy all her very best and sleepiest-sounding special lullabies.

Then she whispered, "Was one of those the right one?"

The only answer was the buzz of snores coming from Fearless Freddy's corner. He was fast asleep.

"It must have been," said Minna. "Goodnight, everyone."

No one answered. Minna heard only the snuffles of a dreaming frog and the soft breathing of a baby in her cradle. She closed her eyes and went to sleep till morning.

*illustrated by Simone Abel*

# Runaway
## *Philippa Pearce*

ONE day Jim woke up feeling ill.

Jim's mother had to go to work. She didn't know what to do: Jim couldn't go to school, and he couldn't stay at home all by himself. In the end, Jim's mother got him out of bed and put on his zip-up bedroom slippers for him and put on his duffel coat over his pyjamas and put a rug round his shoulders and walked him round to Mrs Pratt's house. Mrs Pratt used to mind Jim before he was old enough to go to school.

Jim's mother knocked at Mrs Pratt's front door. Mrs Pratt opened it. She looked surprised and rather cross to see Jim in his bedroom slippers and his pyjamas.

Jim's mother said: "He's not well enough to go to school."

Mrs Pratt said: "I can't look after him today. I'm doing all my washing today."

"Oh, *please*!" said Jim's mother.

"Well," said Mrs Pratt, "he'll have to be very good and not get in my way."

"He'll be as good as gold," said Jim's mother. "He's not himself at all. He doesn't feel well enough to be bad."

So Mrs Pratt agreed to mind Jim; and Jim's mother went off to work.

Jim lay on Mrs Pratt's settee, still in his bedroom slippers and duffel coat, with the rug over him. He listened to Mrs Pratt's washing-machine. In the middle of her washing, Mrs Pratt came to ask if he'd like a cup of tea and some alphabet biscuits. She would make sure there were three biscuits that spelt J-I-M.

"No, thank you," said Jim, as polite as polite, and as good as gold. Mrs Pratt tucked the rug round him and went off again. She was kind when she wasn't worrying about her washing.

He listened some more to Mrs Pratt's washing-machine, and he dozed off.

When he woke up, he remembered about the tea and biscuits, and wished that he hadn't said no. He felt hungry now. He felt better. In fact, he felt quite well again.

He got off the settee and went to look in the kitchen. Mrs Pratt had just finished her washing. She was on her hands and knees, cleaning up a lot of water on the kitchen floor. She was muttering to herself. She sounded cross again. She didn't see Jim.

Jim tiptoed past the kitchen door and looked into the backyard. Mrs Pratt's clean washing was hanging on the washing-line, blowing in the wind. Jim went into the yard to stand with the clean sheets and shirts and other things blowing about him. One of Mr Pratt's shirts flapped its arms at him, teasing him. He tried to catch the shirt. It twisted away from his hands and flapped high in the air, out of his reach. But, in the end, of course, it had to flap down again.

"Got you!" said Jim.

The shirt pulled away from his grip. Jim hung on. The shirt gave a jerk, and Jim gave a big jerk back, just to show it.

And then, in a sudden hurry, the shirt rushed down on him, and all the other washing rushed down as well – right down to the ground. Jim had pulled the washing-line down: all the clean washing lay there on the dirty ground.

Jim was scared at what he'd done. He knew how very cross Mrs Pratt would be. He scuttled back into the house – but quietly. He scuttled quietly past the kitchen door. Mrs Pratt had just finished cleaning the floor. She was beginning to stand up. Then she would look out of the kitchen window into the backyard.

Jim didn't wait for Mrs Pratt to look out of the window. He ran to the front door, and out of it, and went running down the street.

He ran and he ran and he ran. He ran himself out of breath.
Then he stopped for a moment to look behind him: no Mrs Pratt.
So he walked on, but quickly. He thought he knew the way home.
Certainly, it wasn't far. When he got there, he could sit on the
doorstep and wait for his mother to come home from work. If Mrs
Pratt came looking for him, he could hide behind the dustbins.

As Jim walked along, a car overtook him, and stopped. It had
POLICE written along the side. A cheerful voice through the
window said: "Hello, sonny! Where are you off to in your
bedroom slippers and pyjamas?"

Jim ran. He ran and he ran, and he dodged down an alley for
pedestrians only, where the car marked POLICE couldn't follow
him. He heard the policeman shouting "Hi!" behind him.

He ran out of the alleyway and into an ordinary street. He ran
and he ran and he ran. He ran himself out of breath again. Then
he stopped to look behind him: no policeman.

The policeman in the police car must have spotted him because

of his zip-up bedroom slippers and his pyjamas. Jim noticed that people in the street sometimes stared at him, too. Well, he couldn't do anything about his bedroom slippers, but he stopped in a quiet place to roll up the legs of his pyjamas. He rolled them both right up, so that they didn't show underneath his duffel coat any more.

Then he went on; and people seemed not to look at him so much.

He had given up the idea of going straight home, because by now he had no idea where home was. His home couldn't be far away, but all the same Jim was lost. He didn't like the idea of being lost. He tried not to think of it.

He came to a street he did know: Market Street. There were stalls on either side of Market Street, selling fruit and vegetables and fish and meat and china and dress-materials and old magazines and junk of all kinds. Jim had often been to Market Street with his mother. She did most of her shopping here, on her way home from work.

Today, as usual, Market Street was crowded. People with shopping bags went to and fro along the pavements and in the road between the market-stalls. They filled Market Street, so that there was no room for cars to drive down it. There would be no danger to Jim from a car marked POLICE.

So Jim turned down Market Street. He walked past stalls selling fruit and all kinds of other food. He felt very hungry indeed; but he had no money to buy anything.

He went slowly on.

Now it began to rain.

Jim put up the hood of his duffel coat, but water was beginning to soak through the soles of his zip-up bedroom slippers. He thought to himself that he could keep dry if he crept under one of the stalls. He must do that.

But which one?

He decided on a fruit-stall where there was nobody but an old lady choosing some bananas. He stood by the stall. The old lady was looking for the particular bananas she wanted. Jim moved right against the front of the stall. The old lady pointed upwards to where her particular bananas hung, and the stall-keeper looked upwards to where she was pointing. No-one at all was looking at Jim. He stooped quickly and lifted the sacking hanging over the front of the stall and crept underneath.

Underneath the stall was like a dim cave, with some of the space taken up by empty orange-boxes and other rubbish. From a box at the far side of the cave there came a long, bad-tempered growl.

There was a dog. A watch-dog.

Jim nearly went back by the way he had just come, but he knew he might very easily be caught. He decided just to keep as far away from the dog as possible, and be always ready to make a dash for it. As Jim's eyes grew used to the gloom, he could see the dog. It was very old and very fat. It didn't like Jim's being there, but it couldn't be bothered to get up and waddle across to bite him. There was nothing for Jim to do but sit quietly and try not to annoy the dog.

Jim found a pile of old sacks and settled into it. He sat and watched the feet of the people passing on the rainy pavement outside. It might have been cosy for him in his nest of sacks, if he hadn't been lost, and hungry and thirsty.

Sometimes the feet on the pavement stopped at Jim's stall. He could hear the voices of the people buying fruit from the stall-keeper. Fruit! Jim thought longingly of the fruit in the stall just above his head: apples – oranges – pineapples – pears. His mouth watered. In the cave under the stall, there was nothing for Jim to eat, nothing for him to drink. The dog was luckier. It had a bowl of water just under its nose; and, during the afternoon, the stall-keeper's hand came under the sacking with a meaty bone for it.

In the end, Jim fell asleep on his sacks; and he dreamed that he was at home. He dreamed that his mother had made him pancakes for tea. He'd put sugar on the first one, and his mother was saying something about lemon to go with the sugar…

He woke up, and there he was on the sacks, and there were the feet of people passing to and fro on the rainy pavement outside, and somebody had stopped at his stall to buy fruit. He stared and stared at a pair of feet standing there – a woman's feet. Then, suddenly, he heard his mother's voice, almost over his head: "Yes, a lemon, please. Just one lemon. Yes, that lemon will do."

It was Jim's mother – really and truly his mother!

Jim burst out from underneath the stall, the watch-dog barking furiously behind him. He flung himself upon his mother. His mother cried out, and all the shoppers round about exclaimed, and the watch-dog waddled out and bit someone, which made the confusion worse.

Jim began to explain to his mother, but, in the middle of explaining, he burst into tears because he was so hungry and thirsty – and lost. Then the fruit-stall man brought him a cup of tea from somewhere, and someone else gave him a bun to eat, and a junk-stall man dug out a very old push-chair and Jim's mother put him into it. The junk-stall man put a moth-eaten hearth-rug over Jim's knees to keep him warm, and his mother pushed him home. Jim had not been in a push-chair since he'd grown big enough to go to school, but he didn't mind today.

When they got within sight of home, there was Mrs Pratt who looked more worried than she ever looked about her washing; and she had been crying, too, and there was the car marked POLICE as well. Everyone had a lot to say; but Jim's mother took Jim straight indoors and upstairs. She gave him a bath and put him to bed. Then she brought him his tea in bed; it was pancakes with lots of sugar and lemon.

Jim's mother told him how silly he had been to run away from Mrs Pratt's, and how very silly he had been not to let the police help him and bring him home. But she didn't tell him all that until after he had eaten four pancakes with sugar and lemon.

And after that he slept and slept and slept.

*illustrated by Caroline Sharpe*

# THE HEARTLESS GIANT

## *North European folk tale, retold by Anthony Minghella*

ON the whole, there's absolutely no need to be frightened of Giants. Giants are gentle souls, perfectly harmless, and very affectionate. Unless, of course, the Giant has no heart in his body.

Think of all kinds of unpleasant things and add Giant to them and that's what you get when a Giant has no heart. Such a Giant once terrorized a country in the far north of the world, near the very top. He'd hidden his heart. It gave him too much trouble, all those Giant Feelings, too much pain. In its place was a wasps' nest. About to swarm. Put your ear to his chest and you'd hear an angry buzzing noise.

This Heartless Giant could shake a man and shuffle his wits. He could crack a skull with his fist like a walnut. And frequently did. Until, at last, the old King of that country, as good as the Giant was bad, trapped him in a giant trap and locked him in a cell. There the Giant crouched, an inch of outside world to look at, the damp dripping from the walls, the dull rattle of his chains, his low angry growl a ceaseless rumble through the King's castle.

Years passed in this way until the Giant's voice had grated away to the hoarsest whisper and folk had quite forgotten about Giants with no hearts. And he'd be there still, in his foul pit, were it not for a little boy whose name was Leo.

Leo was the King's youngest son. He had two brothers who were bigger. Prince Leo could leave no stone unturned, no passage unexplored, no drawer unrummaged, so incurably curious was he. One morning, scouting the far and deep of the castle, he came across a tiny, barred window set in the bottom of a huge grey wall. Looking through it, Leo saw nothing but dank dark pitch black. But as he turned away he imagined he heard something stir, and then came a growl, a low buzz of a growl. It was a frightening sound.

His brothers told him a Giant with no heart lived in this prison with the tiny window. He didn't believe them. They were older, his brothers, and forever teasing him. But next day he went back, carrying his drum. "Rat-tat-rat-ta-ta-tat," he played outside the window. From inside the dank dark pitch black he heard a rattle, like the rattle of a chain. He crept to the window and squinted into the shadows. Two eyes blinked back at him. Leo jumped. A wasp buzzed angrily through the bars. Leo ran off. It was true, there was a Giant!

All night Leo thought about the Giant, his eyes, the low rumbling growl. Next morning, he was back, "rat-tat-rat-ta-ta-tat!" on his little drum. The Giant was waiting for him. When Leo tiptoed to the window, he was there, whispering hello. The Giant told Leo that long ago he had done some bad things and that the King had locked him up. Leo couldn't imagine what these bad things were. He worried about the poor Giant, stuck down there in terrible chains.

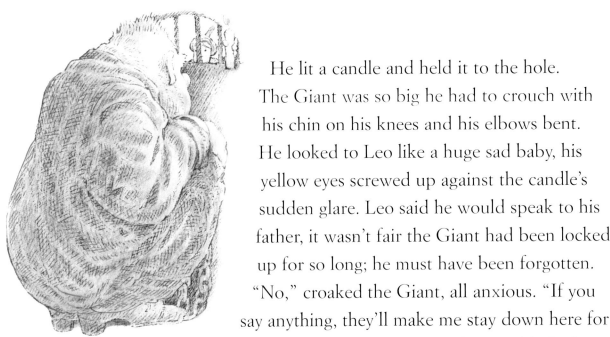

He lit a candle and held it to the hole. The Giant was so big he had to crouch with his chin on his knees and his elbows bent. He looked to Leo like a huge sad baby, his yellow eyes screwed up against the candle's sudden glare. Leo said he would speak to his father, it wasn't fair the Giant had been locked up for so long; he must have been forgotten.

"No," croaked the Giant, all anxious. "If you say anything, they'll make me stay down here for ever and I shall surely perish." The eyes blinked nearer. "Would you like to be my friend?"

Leo was elated. "Oh yes, yes please!"

"Good. Good," said the Giant. Good, thought Leo; I have a secret friend. Good, thought the Giant who had shed his heart; at last. And he sighed a chill sigh and planned chill plans, while the young Prince skipped back along the path, swinging the iron gate behind him, caressing his secret, nurturing it, back to his room.

And so it began, the friendship between the huge, crouching Giant and the little Prince. Every day, the boy would appear, rat-tat-tatting on his drum. Every day, he'd tell a little more, hear a little more, until he felt he knew no-one better, that no-one knew him better. Oh, he wanted to tell the whole world about his friend. But the Giant said, "Our secret," and Leo agreed, although he would have loved to tell his mother or his two brothers or somebody. But he couldn't so he shouldn't, so he wouldn't so he didn't. The Giant, meanwhile, crouched in his blackness and schemed. And so it was that one day he told Leo he'd heard a Guard saying that the King slept with the keys to the Giant's chains hanging on a ring by his bed. Leo had always thought those keys were for the Crown Jewels. "No," said the Giant. "They're for my misery." Leo felt desperate for his misunderstood friend, and a plan formed in his mind. The Giant watched it being born and sighed a cold sigh. Deep inside, in the place where his heart should have been, the wasps seethed and buzzed.

That very night, when the whole castle was sleeping, when the Royal Guards slumped against their sentry posts and dozed, when the owls hooted, little Prince Leo slipped from his bed, slid past a sleeping sentry, and pushed on the door of his parents' room. He tiptoed round the great bed with its velvet eiderdown, past his sleeping mother and sleeping father, to the hook where the keys were hung. They were so heavy. He heaved them up and they swung together, clanging like the Angelus bell. Leo clutched them tight, their black metal teeth squashing his toes, their looped handles framing his face. Slowly, slowly, inch by inch, he dragged the huge keys out of the room.

"I've got the keys," he whispered, trembling at the little window. He let them ring against the bars. "Who goes there?" challenged a voice from the darkness. It was the one sentry still awake. "Hurry, hurry!" growled the Giant from the bowels of the dungeon. Leo struggled to push the keys through the bars.

The teeth went in and the long shafts, but when it came to the ring he couldn't work out how to do it. "They're too big," he explained as he heard the Giant's snort of impatience. "I can't do it." Leo wanted to drop the keys and run for his life. "Push them," hissed the Giant. "Push them!" The Giant's voice was colder than the night, it was icy. Leo pushed. A great hand yanked on the keys. Leo saw its shape in the shadows. He felt a terrible force pulling downward.

"Who goes there?" demanded the approaching voice. And then, with a sudden wrench, the keys disappeared, pulling the bars with them into the blackness. Leo heard a sigh issue from the Giant. A horrible aching sigh. Then the turning of the locks, the crushing of doors. "Don't forget to let me have them back," he said, staring blankly into the dungeon. He shivered again.

The sentry's torch was almost upon him. Suddenly the silence was rent with cries. A man screamed, and there was the sound of crunching, like a great walnut cracking. Then a broken, throaty roar. At the far corner, a door burst from its hinges, spilling light on to Leo's face. The Giant appeared. First his head, squeezing at the entrance, pulling away bricks and lintels, then his shoulders, squeezing, straining through. A giant baby being born into the night. Leo watched, horrified.

The Giant glanced at Leo, but only for a second. As he emerged from the entrance, first one sentry, then a second confronted him, challenging him with sword and spear. The Giant hoisted them up, one in each fist, and cracked their heads together before tossing them away. Then, with the sound of groans and cries proclaiming his release, as the Guards sounded the alarm, the Heartless Giant turned and limped off, roaring his broken roar.

All night Leo sat shivering on the battlements as the King and his men searched the grounds of the castle. His father's angry words haunted him. "Someone betrayed us. Only a madman would help a Giant with no heart. Someone betrayed us." Leo's face swam with tears. So let down, he felt. So stupid. So guilty. Every scream was his fault. Every cracked skull. And when finally morning came, the boy in him, the innocent heart, the joy in him, they were gone – those things, like his friend – and they would never return.

Next morning, Leo looked down and saw his Elder Brother march across the courtyard. He carried his sword and his axe and his bow and a large saddlebag, which he yanked up on to his shoulder. "Where are you going?" Leo called down. "Sh-h-h!" warned his brother. "I am going to get back the Giant." Leo felt awful. "Have you told anybody?" Elder Brother shook his head proudly. "No. Of course not. But I must go. Father is too old." And with this he offered up his hand in salute and turned, young warrior, off to find the Giant. "I'm sorry," wept his brother, but no one heard him.

And Elder Brother did not come back.

The spring came and went with sadness in it. Every day, more stories reached the castle of the Giant's cruel rampage. So it was that one glum morning, perched up on the ledge of his window, Leo looked down and saw Middle Brother striding through the courtyard, golden helmet blazing, shield sparkling. "Where are you going?" Leo called out. "To find our brother and to kill the Giant." Leo was beside himself. "Please don't! It's madness. He has no heart." Middle Brother shook his proud head. "I must go. Our father's too old now." Leo could not stand it. "But he'll trick you!" he blurted out. "He'll trick you!" Middle Brother would not listen. He raised his hand in salute and set off to find the Giant. Terrible, Leo felt, as he watched him go, terrible.

And Middle Brother did not come back either.

The summer that year was short, the winter wild and endless. One day, Leo heard his mother's sobs from far off and came into her bedroom to find her kneeling in sorrow, head against the green velvet of the eiderdown. "Mother?" The Queen did not look up. "Your father says he intends to go off and fight the Giant. I've lost two sons already. He's too old. He's too ill." She wept and wept. She wanted Leo to promise he would never follow his brothers. "Promise me, promise me you won't ever go." But he couldn't promise, how could he? Were it not for him, the Heartless Giant would still be chained and locked and safe in the dungeon.

Next morning, at the crack of dawn, dressed in a thick leather jerkin, Leo stole into the Royal Stables. He carried with him saddlebags stuffed with cheese and ham and biscuits and salted

beef, but no weapon of any kind. He approached the stall where
his father's stallion stood, tall, scarred, imperious, swung the
saddle over the beast's back, and led him from the stable. Off
they rode without looking back, their breath steaming out before
them, the path flashing by, on and on and on.

And so the young Prince Leo rode the land in search of his
once friend the Heartless Giant. Three winters came and went,
their bitter shiver, but still he rode on, determined. And many
times were the saddlebags emptied and filled; many nights slept
achingly cold, huddled with his horse for warmth; many days

spent without sighting a single soul. The boy changed slowly into
man, took his own counsel, his jaw set in resolve, his heart firm,
his plan fixed. Yet to find the Heartless Giant was no easy thing.
His pillage had stripped the landscape bare. Only bleached bones,
spat-out ruins, whispered nightmares remained. Where the Giant
was no-one knew. Long gone, the survivors told Leo as he bent
from the horse's neck. Long gone.

Then one day he came to a place and knew he was finally on
the Giant's trail. The sweet stench of blood curdled the air.

A village, abandoned, smouldered and smoked. Leo's horse reared and bucked and was fearful. Looking down to the earth for clues, they saw a bird flap, helpless, a torn wing shuddering pitifully. The Prince set down and took up the bird in his hands. "Craa! Craa! Help me!" it cried. "The Giant broke me and now I cannot fly, cannot eat. Craa! Help me."

And Leo tended the bird, fixed its wing, fed it bread soaked in milk. And soon all was well with it. Leo threw it high into the air and watched it soar, its vivid re-ascent. "Thank you!" cried the bird from the heavens. "If you need me, I shan't forget." And with a "Craa! Craa!" it flew off. And they followed.

Not long after, Leo stopped at a brook, horse and rider hungry and thirsty, sore and weary. As they drank, they heard a flapping, heard a thrashing, heard a slapping, and, looking round, Leo saw a salmon, twisting, frantic, beached in the crook of a small crevasse. "Help me!" cried the choking fish. "Help me back into the water! I'm stuck here, I'm stranded, I'm beached up and landed! Help me!"

Now Leo was famished, and he loved salmon over the taste of any fish. But he'd suffered sufficient, this fellow, thought the Prince. He picked up the flailing fish and swung it gently into the stream, back to where the salmon is King. Off it flashed through the reeds and green ripples, before leaping up in the middle of the water, slapping the surface with its message. "Thank you!"

it cried. "If you need me, I shan't forget." Then it plunged back into the brook, and they followed its zig and its zag down the stream, for that way lay the Giant.

Now neither Leo nor his horse had eaten for days. They were faint with hunger. Their progress slowed to a weary jog and stumble, until at last the old stallion sank slowly to his knees and gave up the ghost. "Enough," he sighed, rolled over, and died. Leo lay beside his faithful servant and shed tears enough to break a heart, half from love, half from despair. Then he slipped into sleep. He dreamed he was in his mother's bed, warm and cherished. So warm, his mother nursing him, licking up his wet cheeks, hugging him. So vivid. He woke hugging himself, only to find a dead horse beside him and not his mother but a great Wolf coiled around his body, terrible teeth glistening, tongue hanging out with hunger.

And, seeing his eyes flicker, the Wolf howled a terrible howl, fixed on Leo's bare, unguarded throat. "Help!" howled the Wolf. "I've not eaten since the winter came. Help me and I'll not forget you." Leo had no food, save his own flesh. He took up his courage and spoke to the Wolf, whose sour breath plaited with his own, so near they were to the other's jaw. "How can I?" he replied. "I have no food myself." The Wolf nudged against the dead horse. "Then let me eat your horse," he panted, his tongue a vicious red swipe across his teeth. "I'll eat it and be strong again. Trust me. I'll help you."

The Prince could not watch as the starving animal leapt upon the flesh of the stallion. In no time, he'd eaten every scrap of

flesh, chewed the bones, spat them out. Leo
allowed himself a single glance from a
distance. He caught the Wolf's red eyes
contemplating him, the tongue sweeping
the teeth, the body crouched over a
mess of rib and hunk.

"Master. Come here," said the Wolf.
Leo was resigned. "Am I next to go?"
he asked simply. The Wolf nodded.
"Oh yes, us both must go," he
replied. "For you seek the
Giant, I know. And now,
strong again, I'll help you.
On my back, sir, and
let's leave this place."

Off they went a grey dash, a day and a night and a morning,
until they came at last to a strange garden full of statues. Stone
men. Stone women. Stone soldiers. Leo slipped from Greylegs'
back and examined the statues. So lifelike were they, he felt a
warmer sun might thaw them into being. He passed the bent,
supplicant figure of an old woman, ivy in her stone tresses, then
came to a statue of a brave young warrior, sword drawn, shield
raised. Leo walked round to face it. "It's my brother!" he gasped.
"This is a statue of my brother!" Greylegs the Wolf shook his
grey head. "No, my Lord, no statue. This is the Giant's work.
There is his house," he continued, nodding towards a clearing.
"All who approach he turns to stone."

A little way down, the Prince came across another figure, frozen in the act of straining at the longbow, arrow poised at the ear. It was Elder Brother. "You too!" cried Leo in despair. "You too."

At the end of the clearing was the place where the Giant lived, a strange building made by tearing up a whole village and squashing it into a single house. Inside, the Heartless Giant was asleep. A "rat-tat-rat-ta-ta-tat" interrupted his dreams. "Rat-tat-rat-ta-ta-tat," over and over. He heaved his huge frame to the patchwork of windows and looked out. Standing there, fearless, without weapon, beating his child's drum, was the young Prince Leo.

The Giant took Leo in as his servant. The Prince explained how it was discovered he had helped the Giant escape. The Giant laughed at this. Had he seen his brothers, stone men in the garden? Leo said he had. Any who crossed him got the same treatment, so Leo had better be on his mettle. The Giant picked up the drum between his fingers and tapped out the march rhythm, memories flooding back. "That terrible cage," he sighed. "I had to fool you to get the keys. Otherwise I'd still be there, rotting. I still limp, you know." Then he squeezed Leo affectionately in his palm. "So, my little Leo, back again. Hah! Yes, stay if you like. No tricks, though, no traps. Else you'll end up like your brothers."

"No tricks, no traps," agreed the boy and went inside.

So Leo became the servant of the Heartless Giant. For weeks he cleaned, for weeks he scoured, until spick where speck was and span where squalor. Each evening, the Giant returned from his wild outings to find the fire lit, the hearth swept, his breeches pressed. He liked this. Very nice. "Very nice," he'd say as he slurped and slopped his stew. "I should have had a servant before. I like it." He burped. "It befits a Giant." Leo bowed and cleared the plates away. He was always silent, always polite, always cleaning, always watching.

Then the Giant croaked his cracked laugh. "And I don't treat you bad, do I? For a Heartless Giant." Leo kept walking away with the dishes. He spoke without looking back, his words light and idly curious. "What happened to your heart?"

Black clouds furrowed the Giant's brow. "It's in safekeeping," he growled. Leo kept walking. The Giant continued, suddenly swelling, thumping the place where his heart should have been: "Can't feel without it, can I? Can't get hurt. Can't die from heartbreak if I haven't got one. I'm invincible!" he guffawed. Leo shrugged, impressed. "Clever," he said casually. "So where is it, then, your heart?" Wasps streamed from the Giant's mouth. "He who pries is prone to die," he warned. "Do you follow me?"

"Yes." Leo walked into the kitchen. Then the Giant called after him. "But I'll tell you if you want to know. My heart's in that cupboard."

Leo was passing a huge laundry press, its old wooden doors bleached and scarred with age. He paused for an instant, felt his own heart pounding, pounding. There! pounded his heart; his heart is there! The Heartless Giant, crouching at the table, missed nothing. He smirked, belched, and slumped into an after-dinner snore.

Next morning, the Giant stalked off as early as ever. His prison years had made him fearful of walls. Out he went, all the daylight hours, roving, raging, rampaging. Leo stood at the window watching him limp and lumber away. Then he rushed to the linen press, heaved on the doors. Inside was a riot of this and that; a tusk, a trowel, a tent, a trap, a towel, a tin, a thousand trinkets. And then boxes. All manner of boxes. Leo opened them all, big or small. Two were heart-shaped. He tore at them. But there was no heart. Anything but hearts.

"I'm back," announced the Giant later that evening, tossing a brace of dead pigs on the kitchen step. The Giant sniffed into the air. A suspicious sniff. "What's that smell?" he demanded, his nose tilted up, snorting like a bellows. Leo pointed at the gleaming doors of the old cupboard.

"Polish," he said. The Giant's eyes widened in disbelief. "What you polishing the cupboard for?" he demanded.

"It's the home of your heart," declared Leo. "It should be polished." The Giant roared with laughter. "Did you really think I kept my heart in a cupboard? Gah!" Leo feigned a look of disappointment, then went to the first pig and heaved it up on his shoulders to carry into the pantry. It was still warm. "If you want to know," the Giant called after him, "my heart is under the step."

"Right," said Leo, treading on the stone step and continuing on his way. "That old step," chortled the Giant. "That's where my little heart beats. Ticktock."

Next morning, same story: off stomped the Giant and out went the Prince, pick and shovel, hack and hew, digging out the step, spooning out the earth. Stone. Dust. Roots. But no heart! Ach! Poor Leo. He sank down on to the step, feet in the mounds of earth, and despaired. From where he sat he could see the grim silhouettes of his brothers and their fellow sufferers. Waiting.

Waiting for him to make amends.

"I'm back," called the Giant, throwing down a sack, splitting it, and revealing hares and hens and ducks and every type of small bird, all strangled. As he limped into the house, the Giant looked down to see a map of his journey recorded in huge red footprints. "What's that?" he demanded as Leo appeared.

"Ah, you must have trodden on the step, sir," replied Leo politely. "I painted it." The Giant scowled. "What did you paint that old step for?"

"It covers your heart, and should be special." Leo bowed. "What?" guffawed the Giant. "You're a daffle-box! You'd believe anything!"

"Yes," admitted Leo. "I suppose I am, sir. I mean, I fetched you the keys to the dungeon thinking I could trust you, didn't I? So… yes."

The Giant didn't know how to take this. He wasn't sure whether he should feel flattered or insulted. So he sat on his chair and offered his smudged boots for Leo to remove.

"The fact is, no one can find my heart," he declared proudly. "I'll tell you exactly where it is and you'll still not find it." Leo did not look up, but continued unwinding and unwinding the bootlaces as the Giant unleashed a torrent of directions in a single breath. "Far away, so far you could not fathom it, so high you could not climb it, is a mountain, and in the mountain is a lake and in the lake is an island and in the island is a church and in the church is a well and in the well is a duck and in the duck is an egg and in the egg… is my heart." The Giant poked Leo with a giant finger, bowling him over and over on the flagstones. "Not so easy, little thief, eh?" he declared. "Not such a diddle and a doddle as you thought, is it? No. Your father tricked me once. I shan't be tricked again."

That night as the Giant slept, Leo lay on his cot staring at the ceiling. An egg in a duck in a well in a church in an island in a lake in a mountain. Impossible, he decided as he stole from the house and began the journey. Impossible, he decided as he passed his brothers. Impossible, he decided as he glanced at the moon and saw, in its pale silver, his friend Greylegs the Wolf, raising his head to the wind and howling long and loud before turning and bounding towards him. In a second, they were reunited, and Leo was explaining everything. He knew, he said, he knew where the Giant's heart was, he knew how to get there, but the journey was hard, treacherous, impossible.

"Hold tight," said Greylegs, offering the Prince his back. "Hold fast." And very tight the young Prince held, and very fast, for a grey dash they went, headlong, a breathless blur of world flashing by. And they came to the mountain, clambering, scrambling. And up at last. And then the lake. Wide. Deep. "Hold tight!" the Wolf cried again. "Hold close." And plunge, splash into the lake, heads arched up above the water, cold, soaking, chilled, choking. And out at last. On the island.

In its centre loomed the church, its spire so high it threatened to tear Heaven. Leo twisted the iron handles on the massive doors. The doors were locked. Nothing would budge them. Leo hammered in frustration on the thick oak panels. Above them the bells rang for the Angelus. They looked up at the swing and toll.

"Look!" cried Greylegs and, squinting into the glare, Leo saw, dangling impossibly high from the bell tower, the key. Then, mingling with the cling-clang-clang-clong-clang of the bells, came a new note. "Craa!" it sounded. "Craa! Craa!" And from nowhere the bird whose wing Leo had mended swooped past them in salute before swinging up to the tower with a single beat and pulling the key off its thread. Seconds later, the doors swung open. Sure enough, in one corner they came upon a well, and in the well swam a duck.

Leo clambered up on to the lip of the well and began to scatter bread to tempt the duck towards his open hands. He coaxed the duck with each crumb, nearer and nearer until, with a sudden lunge, he had the bird firmly in his grasp. But then, just as he pulled the duck out of the water, the egg dropped from its body back into the water, sinking into the blackness. Leo was dumbfounded. Then, miraculously, the water's skin broke and a beautiful fish leapt, twisted, turned, and plunged, then reappeared slapping the water with its tail. The salmon! Back it dived, vanished, surfaced to flip the egg high into the air. "Catch it!" howled Greylegs at Leo. And he did. He caught the Giant's heart. Held it in his hands.

For a second time, the Heartless Giant woke to the sound of a drum playing. "Rat-tat-rat-ta-ta-tat. Rat-tat-rat-ta-ta-tat." "Where've you been?" he roared in his cracked voice as he charged from the house towards Leo. "I've a good mind to set you there with your brothers." Leo ignored him, continued the little roll on his drum. "Rat-tat-rat-ta-ta-tat. Rat-tat-rat-ta-ta-tat." The Giant boiled. "Stop that!" he ordered. Leo did not stop, but spoke as he continued to beat on the drum. "Years ago, sir, you broke my heart," he said in a quiet voice. "Now I shall break yours." And with that he laid down his drum and held aloft the egg that held the Giant's heart. The Giant was terrified, paralyzed.

"No!" he whispered. "Don't… Be careful… don't break that… please, I beg you." Leo stood before him, the egg pressed threateningly between his palms. "I will break it," he promised. "I'll squeeze and squeeze it to bits unless you release my brothers and all these poor people."

"Yes!" Anything! Don't drop, careful, please, please be careful!" The Giant seemed to shrink with each second, his voice disintegrating to a sorry broken chord. "I'll do anything you ask," he promised, staggering towards the stone figures. "Look! I'm doing it!" And with that he limped from statue to statue, touching each one, mumbling the while. As he passed, each pose melted, softened, shuddered into life. Leo's brothers ran to him, praising Heaven, embracing him. "Brother! You've rescued us!" they cried.

The Giant limped towards the three brothers. "I've done as you bid," he whispered. "Can I have my heart?" Leo nodded. "You can, sir. As I promised. For I know that with your heart in place you could not be as you are now." The Giant sighed. "Thank you," he said, holding out his hand for the return of his heart.

Leo's brothers lunged at him, trapping his arms, snatching the egg from his grasp. Leo yelled. The Giant groaned. "Now, villain!" the brothers cried. "For five long years we've stood here helpless and watched your cruelty." Leo protested, struggled. The Giant hung his head, closed his eyes. "Please," he asked sadly. "Don't. Please." By now, the crowds of liberated souls had surrounded the group, demanding vengeance. "Kill him!" they chanted. "Kill him! Kill him! Kill him!"

"Don't!" Leo pleaded. "I promised! Don't!" But no one heard him. His Elder Brother advanced on the Giant and squeezed on the egg. The Giant staggered back, clutching the place where his heart should have been, gasping for air, short agonized gasps. The crowd roared its approval. Leo wept and wept, screaming to be heard over the cheering. His brother squeezed again. As he sank slowly to his knees, the Giant caught Leo in a terrible gaze. "You promised," he said. "You promised."

Then the egg burst in the elder Prince's hands, yolk and white slopping on him. The crowd cheered. The Giant slumped forward and died. Wasps swarmed angrily from his mouth. Where the Giant fell a hill grew. And in time, when much was forgotten, when many Kings had come and gone, the place was still known as the Hill of the Heartless Giant.

Prince Leo lived to be a great age, became King, had forty-two grandchildren, and told them all that tale. But in his story the Giant got back his heart and made amends for all his wrongs. Because, you see, despite all that took place, a little boy once met a Giant and they became friends.

*illustrated by Inga Moore*

# THE BOY WITH TWO SHADOWS
## *Margaret Mahy*

THERE was a little boy who took great care of his shadow. He was quite a careful little boy with his buttons and shoes and all the odd pieces. But most especially he was careful with his shadow because he knew he had only one, and it had to last him his life. He always tried to manage things so that his shadow didn't trail in the dust, and if he just couldn't keep it out of the dust he hurried to get to a clean place for it.

This boy took such care of his shadow that a witch noticed it. She stopped the boy on his way home from school.

"I've been watching you," she said. "I like the way you look after your shadow."

"Well," said the boy, trying to sound grown-up, "the way I see it is this – it's the only one I've got. And it's going to have to last me a long time."

"True! True!" said the witch, looking at him with great approval. "You're the lad for me. The thing is, I want someone to look after *my* shadow while I am away on holiday.

I don't want to drag that skinny old thing around with me. You know what a nuisance a shadow can be."

"Mine isn't any trouble," said the boy doubtfully.

"That's as may be," the witch declared. "The thing is, I want to be rid of mine for two weeks, but I'm not going to leave it with just anybody – it's going to be left with *you*."

The boy didn't like to argue with a witch.

"All right," he said, "but hurry back, won't you?"

The witch bared her teeth in a witch smile, which was quite wicked-looking, though she was trying to be pleasant.

"If you return my shadow in good condition," she promised, "you shall have a magic spell all of your own. I'll choose just the right one for you." Then she fastened her shadow onto the boy's shadow, got on her broom, and made off, light and free as thistledown, with sunlight all around her and no bobbling black patch chasing at her heels.

The boy now had two shadows. One was his own. The other was the fierce, crooked, thorny shadow of the witch.

The boy had nothing but trouble with that witch's shadow. It was the worst behaved shadow in the world! Usually, it is a rule that shadows behave much as their people do – but the witch's wouldn't do that. When the little boy went to buy apples the witch's shadow rummaged among the shadows of the fruit. It put the shadows of all the oranges over beside the bananas, and mixed up the shadows of the peaches. Everything was all higgledy-piggledy.

The man in the fruit shop said, "Throw that shadow out! How on earth am I going to sell oranges when they've got no shadows? And who's going to buy bananas with the shadows of oranges?" The little boy didn't like to turn the witch's shadow loose on its own. He rushed out of the shop without his apples.

At home, all through tea, the witch's shadow stretched itself long and leaped all over the wall. It took the shadow from the clock, and the clock stopped. Then it terrified the parrot into fits, and pulled the shadow-tail of the dog's shadow.

"Really!" said the little boy's mother. "I can't enjoy my tea with that ugly thing waltzing around the walls! You'll have to keep it outside."

But the boy was determined to look after the witch's shadow. From then on, he had his tea in the kitchen on his own. He got so clever at keeping the witch's shadow from getting into mischief and wickedness that at last it couldn't find anything wicked to do. Naturally this made it very cross.

Then suddenly, in spite of the little boy's care, the shadow thought of something new and mean – so mean that you would think even a witch's shadow would be ashamed. It started to pinch and tease and bite and haunt the little boy's own shadow. It was terrible to see. The boy's shadow had always been treated kindly. His own shadow did not know what to do now about this new, fierce thing that tormented it, pushed it onto dusty places and trod on its heels as they hurried down the road.

One day the boy's shadow could bear this no longer. In broad daylight the boy, going home to lunch, saw his two shadows – short and squat – running beside him. He saw the witch's shadow nip his own smaller shadow with her long witch fingernails. His own shadow gave a great bound and broke away from his feet. Down the road it flew, like a great black beetle or a bit of waste paper flapping in the wind, then it was gone. The little boy ran

after it, but it was nowhere to be seen. He stood still and listened to the warm summer afternoon. It was so quiet he could hear the witch shadow laughing – or rather, he heard the echo of laughing. (Because, as you know, an echo is the shadow of a sound, and sometimes the sound of a shadow.)

Well, you can just imagine. There was the little boy with only one shadow again – but it was the *wrong* shadow. His real shadow was quite gone, and now he had only the witch's left.

It was more like having a thorn bush at his heels than a proper shadow. There was nothing comfortable about this, and people stared and nudged one another.

As for the boy, he felt sad and lonely without his own shadow. He tried to like the witch's shadow, and he tried hard to take good care of it – but it was a thankless task. You might just as well try to pet a wild she-wolf or a thistle!

At last the witch came back. She wrote the boy a letter in grey ink on black paper, telling him to meet her that night at midnight and to be sure to bring her shadow with him. (Thank goodness it was a bright moonlit night or it might have been extremely difficult to find that wretched shadow, which hid away from him sometimes.) As it was, the witch whisked it back in half a minute less than no time. (In fact, it didn't even take her as long as that.)

"Now," the witch said very craftily, "here's your spell." She handed the boy a small striped pill, wrapped in a bat's wing.

"It's one I don't use much myself," she said. "But the boy who swallows that pill can turn himself into a camel. *Any* sort of camel, even a white racing camel – or a Bactrian or any sort of camel you like."

The little boy couldn't help feeling it was a bit useless, in a way, to be able to turn himself into a camel. What he really wanted was just his own shadow back. He pointed out to the witch that her fierce shadow had driven his own gentle one away. The witch sniggered a bit in a witch-like, but very irritating, fashion.

"Well, my dear," she said, "you can't expect everything to be easy, you know. Anyhow, I feel I've paid you handsomely for your trouble. Run off home now."

The boy *had* to do what he was told. He scuttled off sadly down the street to his home, carefully holding down the pocket where he had put the striped pill. It was bright moonlight and everything had its shadow – the trees trailed theirs out over the road, the fence posts pointed theirs across the paddocks. The sleeping cows had sleeping shadows tucked in beside them. Only the little boy had no shadow. He felt very lonely.

At the gate to his house, he thought at first that his mother was waiting for him. A dim figure seemed to be watching out, peering up the road. But it wasn't tall enough to be his mother, and besides, when he looked again it wasn't there. Then something moved without any sound. He looked again. Softly and shyly as if it was ashamed of itself, his own shadow slid out from among the other shadows, and sidled towards him. It slipped along, toe-to-toe with him, just as it had always done.

The little boy thought for a moment:

He was free of the witch's shadow.

He had a magic trick that would turn him into any sort of camel he liked – if he ever wanted to.

And now he had his own shadow back again! Everything had turned out for the best. He was so pleased he did a strange little dance in the moonlight, while, toe-to-toe, his shadow danced beside him.

*illustrated by Greg Becker*

# MRS MALLABY'S BIRTHDAY
## Helen Earle Gilbert

THERE was once an old lady who was very, very old. She was so old that she didn't even know herself how old she really was. Her name was Mrs Mallaby, and she lived all alone in a little brick house with a green door, seven windows, and a pretty bright garden growing all around it.

One morning as Mrs Mallaby was finishing her breakfast she heard a knock. "That's the postman," said Mrs Mallaby. "There must be a letter!" So she hurried to the door.

There was the postman, in his blue coat. "Good morning, Mrs Mallaby," he said. "I believe I have something for you this morning." And he began to hunt through his bag.

"Good morning, Mr Walker," said Mrs Mallaby. "Oh, what will it be?"

"Here it is," said the postman.

Sure enough. There was a little blue envelope with a stamp, and it said: *Mrs Mallaby.*

Mrs Mallaby was much excited. She did not often have any mail. She thanked Mr Walker, took the letter into the house, and opened it. Inside there was a pretty card with flowers and a ribbon on it and a message that said: *Happy Birthday, Mrs Mallaby! Many Happy Returns of the Day!*

"It must be my birthday!" Mrs Mallaby said.

She put the card up on the mantel and sat down to count. She counted for nearly an hour. Then she said, "I do believe I'm a hundred years old today. My goodness, how time flies! Well, I rather wish I had a kitten."

Just then there was another knock at the door. Mrs Mallaby hurried to open it.

There stood the neighbour who lived next door – Mrs Bowe. She was holding a large package carefully in both hands.

"Many happy returns of the day, Mrs Mallaby!" said Mrs Bowe. "I've brought you a little remembrance for your birthday."

"How very sweet of you," said Mrs Mallaby. "*I hope it's a kitten.*"

She said the last words very low, to herself, so that Mrs Bowe wouldn't know she was disappointed if it wasn't a kitten.

Mrs Bowe set the package on the table and took off the wrappings. Inside was an enormous birthday cake, with one hundred candles on it.

"Oh, thank you, Mrs Bowe!" cried Mrs Mallaby. "How very nice of you!"

Mrs Bowe was pleased. "We'll light the candles," she said, "and then it'll look quite pretty." So Mrs Mallaby got the matchbox and she and Mrs Bowe lighted the one hundred candles.

"You must have the first piece," she said to Mrs Bowe.

She cut Mrs Bowe quite a large piece of the birthday cake. Then she took a piece herself.

"It's just lovely!" she said. "I've never had such a beautiful cake before."

They sat down and ate their pieces of cake to the last crumb. It was delicious. Then Mrs Bowe said "Good-bye" and "Happy Birthday" and went home.

Then Mrs Mallaby went around her house as she did every day to see that everything was clean and in order.

She washed the dishes and put them away. Then she heard another knock on the door.

She hurried to the door, and who should it be but Dr Blight, another neighbour who lived down the street. Dr Blight was holding a very large, interesting-looking package tightly under one arm.

"How do you do?" he said. "Well, well, well!" (He always said that, even when people were sick.) "I hear you're a hundred! Well, well, well! Many happy returns, Mrs Mallaby, and here's a little birthday present for you!"

Mrs Mallaby ran to get her glasses.

"*Perhaps it will be the kitten this time*," she said to herself. Inside the wrappings was a handsome green silk umbrella, with a bird for a handle.

"Why, how pretty!" cried Mrs Mallaby. "How did you know just what I wanted to take to church on rainy Sundays! Thank you very much, Doctor. Really, I wanted an umbrella more than anything else *except a kitten*."

Mrs Mallaby said the last words to herself, very low. She didn't want to hurt the kind doctor's feelings or let him see that she was disappointed.

"You must have a piece of my birthday cake," she said.

So Mrs Mallaby gave the doctor quite a large piece of her birthday cake. And he said, "Well, well, well!" again and "Thank you!" and went away.

"Well, well, well!" said Mrs Mallaby to herself. "If I couldn't have a kitten, of course I would rather have a birthday cake with a hundred candles and a green silk umbrella with a bird for a handle than anything else there is in the world."

She had no sooner said this than there came another rap at the door. There stood Peter, the little boy who lived across the street.

"Happy birthday, Mrs Mallaby!" shouted Peter. He was holding his hands behind him.

"Why, hello, Peter," said Mrs Mallaby. She was greatly pleased. "How in the world did you know it was my birthday?"

"I have a present for you!" cried Peter. He drew it out from behind him. It was a large bundle wrapped in paper.

Mrs Mallaby's heart began to beat very fast. *Perhaps it would be a kitten.*

"Bring it right in," she cried, "and we'll open it."

They put the bundle on the floor. Peter danced about while Mrs Mallaby untied the string. Inside was a big pasteboard box. Mrs Mallaby lifted the cover. There was a beautiful big wooden boat.

"Why, *Peter*!" said Mrs Mallaby. She was so astonished that she could not say another word.

"I made it myself," said Peter. "I made it in school and painted it too. It's for your birthday."

He took it out of the box and held it up for Mrs Mallaby to see.

"It's made out of two blocks of wood. You put one on top of the other and pound them together with nails," he explained. "There are two smoke-stacks – look! And a string to pull it by. I'll come and sail it for you sometimes if you want me to."

"How beautiful it is!" said Mrs Mallaby. "And to think that you made it yourself."

"It wasn't very hard," said Peter.

"I never thought I should have a boat like this," said Mrs Mallaby. "Would you like a piece of my birthday cake, Peter?"

"Yes, thank you," said Peter. "What a lot of candles! On my birthday I had six."

Peter ate a large piece of cake and then said good-bye.

"You don't know where I could get a kitten, do you, Peter?" asked Mrs Mallaby.

"No," said Peter. "I wish I had one myself. Good-bye."

Then there was quite a long while when nobody came.

But just as Mrs Mallaby was watering her geraniums, she heard another rap at the door. She hurried to open it. There on the step stood the postman's wife, looking very smiling. She was holding a package.

"Happy Birthday!" she said. "I've been planning a little present for your birthday, Mrs Mallaby, and here it is. Many happy returns of the day."

"Why, Mrs Walker," Mrs Mallaby said, "how very nice of you!" She looked at the box her neighbour was holding and her eyes grew bright. She felt happy.

"*I do believe it's a…*" And Mrs Mallaby stopped just in time, for while she was talking she had untied the ribbon and out of the box tumbled a beautiful hand-made apron.

"Why, dear me!" cried Mrs Mallaby. "What a beautiful apron it is! Blue, with red squares. I am so fond of blue. And I do believe there is a pocket!"

She bent over it hastily to look at the stitches, for she didn't want her good friend Mrs Walker to see the tears in her eyes. But she really did want a kitten more and more. The more she thought about it the more she felt she just *must* have a kitten.

"Won't you have a piece of my birthday cake, Mrs Walker?" she asked. "Mrs Bowe made it for me."

"Oh, thank you," replied Mrs Walker, looking admiringly at the beautiful cake with roses and hills of sugar and green leaves around the edge and what were left of the one hundred candles.

So Mrs Mallaby cut a piece of cake for Mrs Walker, and she went away saying "Thank you very much," and that she thought it was going to rain later on in the day.

And now it was time for Mrs Mallaby to get her lunch. She decided to have crisp bacon, two fried eggs, corn bread, gingerbread, and tea – and a little blackberry jam. Just as she was about to sit down, what should she hear but another knock at the door! She was quite excited!

And there stood Mr Cobb, the grocer! He had taken off his white coat and put on his Sunday one, which was black and had tails going down behind. And he had on a shiny derby hat. And he was carrying in his hand a little basket, a covered basket, which he was holding high and carefully.

Mrs Mallaby tried hard not to look at the basket, but her heart kept saying, "*It's a kitten basket. If ever I saw a kitten basket in my life that's a kitten basket!*"

Her fingers trembled and she could hardly hear what the grocer was saying.

"Mrs Mallaby," he was saying, "you've been a good customer to me for many more years than I can remember. Mrs Bowe told me it is your birthday and that you are a hundred years old. When I told that to my wife, she said we must certainly make you a little present." And he lifted the basket and held it out to Mrs Mallaby.

Mrs Mallaby could hardly wait to peer under the cover. When she saw what was there she almost cried. Inside the basket was a neat little package wrapped in white tissue paper and tied with a big silver bow. It couldn't possibly be a kitten!

She turned away so Mr Cobb couldn't see how much she had hoped it would be a kitten.

But Mrs Mallaby was very brave, and she was also very polite (which was why she had so many friends, really) and so she said, "Thank you, Mr Cobb," and, "Won't you have a piece of my birthday cake?"

Then at last she opened the package, and what was inside? Why, a handsome sugar bowl with silver handles and a silver top!

Mrs Mallaby was tremendously surprised. She stared at it and lifted the cover. It was full of lumps of sugar. "It's lovely!" she said. "It was so nice of you and Mrs Cobb to remember me. A sugar bowl – think of it!"

About two o'clock that afternoon, after Mrs Mallaby had finished her lunch and done the dishes and put them away and the kitchen was as clean as a new pin, she sat down by the fire and looked at her presents.

She laid them all out on the table and looked at each one.

There was the pretty birthday card with flowers and a ribbon on it.

There was all that was left of the enormous birthday cake with the one hundred candles, the roses and hills of sugar, and green leaves around the edge.

There was the handsome green silk umbrella with the bird for a handle.

There was the beautiful big wooden boat with two smoke-stacks.

And there was the lovely glass sugar bowl with silver handles and a silver top, and full of lumps of sugar.

"They are very, very nice," said Mrs Mallaby. And because she was such a polite little old lady she would not even let herself think, "*I did want a kitten!*"

Then, because she was really a hundred years old and very sleepy, Mrs Mallaby began to nod a little. She leaned forward in her chair and dozed off into a nap.

It began to rain. The rain beat down steadily against the windows.

And as Mrs Mallaby was dreaming, she heard a little sound:

"M-iaow! M-iaow! M-iaow!"

Mrs Mallaby awoke with a jerk. "What's that?" she said. "Was I dreaming? Have I been asleep?"

She looked all around. There was nothing to be seen and nothing to be heard but the sound of the rain against the windows. Her eyes began to close once more.

Then suddenly she heard it again.

"Mi-a-o-w! Mi-a-o-o-o-w!" very faint and wet and lonesome.

Mrs Mallaby ran to the door and threw it open. There on the doorstep in the rain stood a little black and white kitten. He looked right up at Mrs Mallaby and said, "Mi-a-o-o-w! Mi-a-o-o-w! Mi-a-o-o-w!"

"Well, bless your heart," cried Mrs Mallaby. "Did you come on my birthday to live with me?"

And the kitten said, "Mi-a-o-w, Mi-a-o-o-w, Mi-a-o-o-w!" which meant that he had.

So Mrs Mallaby took him into the house and dried him with a clean towel. She ran into the pantry and got a white bowl with roses on it and filled it with milk. The kitten drank all the milk. Then Mrs Mallaby fixed a basket for him to sleep in.

The kitten said, "Mi-a-o-o-w!" and Mrs Mallaby said, "What a beautiful birthday!"

And from that day to this, Mrs Mallaby and the kitten have lived happily together in the little brick house with the green door, seven windows, and a garden all around.

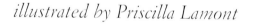

*illustrated by Priscilla Lamont*

# THE GIRL AND THE CROCODILE
## *Leila Berg*

THIS is a story about a promise. And this is the way *I* tell it.

Once upon a time there was a girl who was sitting on a big stone by the river, and watching the fish. And while she was watching, she felt someone was watching *her*. You know how you do?

She looked up, and there was a crocodile. Staring. The little girl wasn't the least bit bothered. She just stared back.

"I bet you can't catch fish," said the girl.

"Oh, easy-peasy!" said the crocodile. "Of course I can."

"Catch me some," said the little girl.

"All right," said the crocodile. "But you'll have to give me something if I do."

Well, the girl thought.

"I don't mind," she said. "On Saturday, my Dad's having a birthday party, and if you come in the morning before it starts I'll give you a bottle of beer."

"Oh, terrific!" said the crocodile. "That's what I really do like!"

He caught a fish for the girl, and one for her Mum and one for her Dad, and she thanked him most politely like her mother had always taught her, and said, "Don't forget now, will you? Saturday's the day" – never thinking for a moment he'd remember. And off she went.

And the crocodile stayed in the river, crossing off his calendar every morning, and saying, "Today's Monday." "Today's Tuesday." "Today's Wednesday." "Today's Thursday." "Today's Friday." "Today's Saturday. *Birthday Party*!"

And out he came, ever so excited, and swished his tail up the High Street, past the café, past the sweet shop, past the place where they sell cars in matchboxes, and into the little girl's street, and he knocked at the door with his tail. Frump! Frump!

The girl came to the door, because there was no one else in the house. Her Mum and Dad were out getting things for the party.

"Oh!" she said. "Oh! I never thought..!"

Well, you don't, do you?

"I've come for my present," said the crocodile.

"Oh, come in, come in," she said, all in a fluster. "Don't stand there on the step. I'll get into terrible trouble."

So he came in, trying quite truly not to knock everything down with his strong tail, which was difficult because the kitchen was small.

And the girl kept saying, "Be quiet! Oh, mind that cup!"

Then the girl got a bottle of beer from a box under the sink, and he emptied it down his throat with a plopping sound. Perlopp. Perlopp. Perlopp.

And when the last drop had gone down, he began to sing a little song.

> *"Crocodiles are not really bad,*
> *Sometimes they're happy and sometimes they're sad.*
> *Whoops!"*

"Oh, do be quiet!" said the girl. "I shall get into terrible trouble if my Mum and Dad hear you."

"But I like singing," said the crocodile. "People always sing at parties. Give me some more beer."

"There isn't any more," she said.

"Oh, you story!" he said. "There are hundreds of bottles under the sink. I *saw* them."

So she gave him another bottle to keep him quiet, and he gurgled that one down too. Perlopp. Perlopp.

And he sang again:

> *"Crocodiles are not really bad,*
> *Sometimes they're happy and sometimes they're sad.*
> *Whoops!"*

"Oh, for heaven's sake be *quiet*!" she said. "We'll have everyone here in a minute, and won't they be mad at me!"

"Well, give me another bottle," he said. So she gave him another.

And he gurgled that one down too, and sang again, beating time with his tail on the dinner-gong that the little girl's Dad had picked up at an auction last Wednesday.

*"Crocodiles are not really bad,*
*Sometimes they're happy and sometimes they're sad.*
*Whoops!"*

And then he wandered out of the house, dancing on his hind legs, and clapping with his front feet, and bumping into the chrysanthemums that the girl's Dad had planted last Sunday.

And the little girl ran after him, crying, "Oh, do be quiet! You'll get me into terrible trouble!"

And just as he went past the pond, the girl managed to push him in. But he got out, and she pushed him in again, and he got out again, and began to chase her right down the street, and past the place where you get the little cars in matchboxes, and past the sweet shop, *and* past the café. And he was singing:

*"Crocodiles are not really bad,*
*Sometimes they're happy and sometimes they're sad.*
*Whoops!"*

and she was shouting (well, you would, wouldn't you?) right down
to the bottom of the hill.

Now all the Mums and Dads were coming out of their gates to
go to her Dad's birthday party, because it was nearly time, you see.

And her Auntie was there. And her Auntie was very sensible
and brave and quick-thinking, and she spread out her arms wide
and stood right in his path, to stop him chasing the girl (whose
name, by the way, was Amanda).

But it was no use. The crocodile just floppered her down with
his tail, giving her a headache for weeks, and went on chasing.

But Amanda's Mum and Dad, who were just coming out of the
cake shop, and all the other Mums and Dads coming out of their
gates, heard the *extraordinary* noise, and came rushing up, and
they stood one behind the other, and they caught the crocodile in
all their hands, and they held him up in the air high above their
heads, and they ran down with him to the river, and they threw
him in. Flup splash!

Then they all came back to the girl, puffing a little, and her Mum and Dad said, "Whatever were you doing with that crocodile? Now tell the truth!"

And the girl said, "Well, you know those fishes we ate on Sunday. Well, that crocodile caught them for me, and I promised I'd give him some beer as a present."

"*You promised him some beer*!" said all the Mums and Dads.

(And her Auntie said, "Oh my poor head!")

And her Mum and Dad said, "Amanda! Don't you know that we never ask crocodiles to parties!"

And all night long, when the party was finished, and all the people gone home, and the last gate shut again, they could hear the old crocodile still singing away to himself in the river, beating time with his tail on the big stone and clapping his front feet.

*"Crocodiles are not really bad,*
*Sometimes they're happy and sometimes they're sad.*
*Whoops!"*

Snip snap snover,
That story's over.

*illustrated by Frank Rodgers*

# TEDDY ROBINSON'S NIGHT OUT
## *Joan Robinson*

TEDDY Robinson was a nice, big, comfortable, friendly teddy bear. He had light brown fur and kind brown eyes, and he belonged to a little girl called Deborah. He was Deborah's favourite teddy bear, and Deborah was Teddy Robinson's favourite little girl, so they got on very well together, and wherever one of them went the other one usually went too.

One Saturday afternoon Teddy Robinson and Deborah looked out of the window and saw that the sun was shining and the almond tree in the garden was covered with pink blossom.

"That's nice," said Deborah. "We can play out there. We will make our house under the little pink tree, and you can get brown in the sun, Teddy Robinson."

So she took out a little tray with the dolls' tea-set on it, and a blanket to sit on, and the toy telephone in case anyone rang them up, and she laid all the things out on the grass under the tree. Then she fetched a colouring book and some chalks for herself, and a book of nursery rhymes for Teddy Robinson.

Deborah lay on her tummy and coloured the whole of an elephant and half a Noah's Ark, and Teddy Robinson stared hard at a picture of Humpty-Dumpty and tried to remember the words. He couldn't really read, but he loved pretending to.

"Hump, hump, humpety-hump," he said to himself over and
over again; and then "Hump, hump, humpety-hump, Deborah's
drawing an elephump."

"Oh, Teddy Robinson," said Deborah, "don't think so loud – I
can't hear myself chalking." Then, seeing him still bending over
his book, she said, "Poor boy, I expect you're tired. It's time for
your rest now." And she laid him down on his back so that he
could look up into the sky.

At that moment there was a loud *rat-tat* on the front door and a
long ring on the door-bell. Deborah jumped up and ran indoors
to see who it could be, and Teddy Robinson lay back and began
to count the number of blossoms he could see in the almond-tree.
He couldn't count more than four because he only had two arms
and two legs to count on, so he counted up to four a great many
times over, and then he began counting backwards, and the
wrong way round, and any way round that he could think of, and
sometimes he put words in between his counting, so that in the
end it went something like this:

> *"One, two, three, four,*
> *someone knocking at the door,*
> *One, four, three, two,*
> *open the door and how d'you do?*
> *Four, two, three, one,*
> *isn't it nice to lie in the sun?*
> *One, two, four, three,*
> *underneath the almond-tree."*

And he was very happy counting and singing to himself for quite a long time.

Then Teddy Robinson noticed that the sun was going down and there were long shadows in the garden. It looked as if it must be getting near bedtime.

Deborah will come and fetch me soon, he thought; and he watched the birds flying home to their nests in the trees above him.

A blackbird flew quite close to him and whistled and chirped, "Good night, teddy bear."

"Good night, bird," said Teddy Robinson and waved an arm at him.

Then a snail came crawling past.

"Are you sleeping out tonight? That will be nice for you," he said. "Good night, teddy bear."

"Good night, snail," said Teddy Robinson, and he watched it crawl slowly away into the long grass.

She will come and fetch me soon, he thought. It must be getting quite late.

But Deborah didn't come and fetch him. Do you know why? She was fast asleep in bed!

This is what had happened. When she had run to see who was knocking at the front door, Deborah had found Uncle Michael standing on the doorstep. He had come in his new car, and he said there was just time to take her out for a ride if she came quickly, but she must hurry because he had to get into the town before tea-time. There was only just time for Mummy to get Deborah's coat on and wave good-bye before they were off. They had come home ever so much later than they meant to because they had tea out in a shop, and then on the way home the new car had suddenly stopped and it took Uncle Michael a long time to find out what was wrong with it.

By the time they reached home Deborah was half asleep, and Mummy had bundled her into bed before she had time to really wake up again and remember about Teddy Robinson still being in the garden.

He didn't know all this, of course, but he guessed something unusual must have happened to make Deborah forget about him.

Soon a little wind blew across the garden, and down fluttered some blossom from the almond tree. It fell right in the middle of Teddy Robinson's tummy.

"Thank you," he said, "I like pink flowers for a blanket."

So the almond tree shook its branches again, and more and more blossoms came tumbling down.

The garden tortoise came tramping slowly past.

"Hallo, teddy bear," he said. "Are you sleeping out? I hope you won't be cold. I felt a little breeze blowing up just now. I'm glad I've got my house with me."

"But I have a fur coat," said Teddy Robinson, "and pink blossom for a blanket."

"So you have," said the tortoise. "That's lucky. Well, good night," and he drew his head into his shell and went to sleep close by.

The next-door kitten came padding softly through the grass and rubbed against him gently.

"You *are* out late," she said.

"Yes, I think I'm sleeping out tonight," said Teddy Robinson.

"Are you?" said the kitten. "You'll love that. I did it once. I'm going to do it a lot oftener when I'm older. Perhaps I'll stay out tonight."

But just then a window opened in the house next door and a voice called, "Puss! Puss! Puss! Come and have your fish! fish! fish!" and the kitten scampered off as fast as she could go.

Teddy Robinson heard the window shut down and then everything was quiet again.

The sky grew darker and darker blue, and soon the stars came out. Teddy Robinson lay and stared at them without blinking, and they twinkled and shone and winked at him as if they were surprised to see a teddy bear lying in the garden.

And after a while they began to sing to him, a very soft and sweet and far-away little song, to the tune of Rock-a-bye Baby, and it went something like this:

*"Rock-a-bye Teddy, go to sleep soon.*
*We will be watching, so will the moon.*
*When you awake with the dew on your paws*
*Down will come Debbie and take you indoors."*

Teddy Robinson thought that was a lovely song, so when it was
finished he sang one back to them. He sang it in a grunty voice
because he was rather shy, and it went something like this:

*"This is me*
*under the tree,*
*the bravest bear you ever did see.*
*All alone,*
*so brave I've grown,*
*I'm camping out on my very own."*

The stars nodded and winked and twinkled to show that they
liked Teddy Robinson's song, and then they sang Rock-a-bye
Teddy all over again, and he stared and stared at them until he
fell asleep.

Very early in the morning a blackbird whistled, then another
blackbird answered, and then all the birds in the garden opened
their beaks and twittered and cheeped and sang. And Teddy
Robinson woke up.

One of the blackbirds hopped up with a worm in his beak.

"Good morning, teddy bear," he said. "Would
you like a worm for your breakfast?"

"Oh, no, thank you," said Teddy Robinson. "I don't usually bother about breakfast. Do eat it yourself."

"Thank you, I will," said the blackbird, and he gobbled it up and hopped off to find some more.

Then the snail came slipping past.

"Good morning, teddy bear," he said. "Did you sleep well?"

"Oh, yes, thank you," said Teddy Robinson.

The next-door kitten came scampering up, purring.

"You lucky pur-r-son," she said, as she rubbed against Teddy Robinson. "Your fur-r is damp but it was a pur-r-fect night for staying out. I didn't want to miss my fish supper last night, otherwise I'd have stayed with you. Pur-r-haps I will another night. Did you enjoy it?"

"Oh, yes," said Teddy Robinson. "You were quite right about sleeping out. It was lovely."

The tortoise poked his head out and blinked.

"Hallo," he said. "There's a lot of talking going on for so early in the morning. What is it all about? Oh, good morning, bear. I'd forgotten you were here. I hope you had a comfortable night." And before Teddy Robinson could answer he had popped back inside his shell.

Then a moment later Teddy Robinson heard a little shuffling noise in the grass behind him, and there was Deborah out in the garden with bare feet, and in her pyjamas!

She picked him up and hugged him and kissed him and whispered to him very quietly, and then she ran through the wet grass and in at the kitchen door and up the stairs into her own room. A minute later she and Teddy Robinson were snuggled down in her warm little bed.

"You poor, poor boy," she whispered as she stroked his damp fur. "I never meant to leave you out all night. Oh, you poor, poor boy."

But Teddy Robinson whispered back, "I aren't a poor boy at all. I was camping out, and it was lovely." And then he tried to tell her all about the blackbird, and the snail, and the tortoise, and the kitten, and the stars. But because it was really so very early in the morning, and Deborah's bed was really so very warm and cosy, they both got drowsy; and before he had even got to the part about the stars singing their song to him both Teddy Robinson and Deborah were fast asleep.

*And that is the end of the story about how Teddy Robinson stayed out all night.*

*illustrated by Brita Granström*

# A Drink of Water

## *John Yeoman*

IT WAS a terribly hot day in the jungle, and all the birds and beasts, exhausted from the heat, had curled up to sleep. The silence was broken only by an occasional snapping of twigs and beating of soft-feathered wings as a parrot nearly slipped off its perch in a tall tree.

The only creature who couldn't sleep was a small brown monkey, who was very very thirsty indeed. He wandered on all fours through the lush green undergrowth in the hope of finding a small puddle. Every now and then he stopped and raised himself on to his back legs, peering this way and that for a tell-tale sparkle of sunlight on water. But it was useless, for it had been a very very long, hot, dry summer.

At last his search led him to the edge of the dark green jungle, to the place where the desert begins. He stopped again, blinking into the strong sunlight. But he knew that there was no chance at all of finding cool water in the desert.

But what was that he could see? Out there, standing all by itself, was a tall, fat pot – just the sort of pot which might be expected to have water in it. With a bound the monkey was beside it. If he climbed on to a dead branch among the stones he could just manage to peer into the dark inside of the pot.

Was there water in it? He couldn't see any water, but then, it was very dark in there. Gingerly he lowered a thin arm into the pot. His long sensitive fingers could feel a coolness which might mean that there was water farther down. So he very carefully lowered his hand farther, and farther, and farther, until he was standing on tiptoe and his arm was stretched as far as it would go. And then the very tips of his long fingers felt cold water. And now what was he to do, may I ask? Just think: the water was so near, and yet so hard to reach!

"I will put my shoulder to the pot," said the small brown monkey, gently scratching his lower lip with a long finger, "and I will rock it until it tumbles over – and then I will drink the water." And he put his thin bony shoulder against the pot, and pushed with all his might. Then he pushed again and again and again until – the pot began to rock. It rocked very little at first but gradually it swayed more and more and it seemed that the very next push would send it toppling over.

"Stop!" called a small voice. The small brown monkey stopped in surprise, and the pot gently rocked itself to a standstill. There was no one to be seen.

"Who said that?" asked the small brown monkey.

"I did," said a green lizard, sliding quickly from beneath the pot and raising his head towards the monkey. "I live under this pot and I was trying to have a nap when you came and started making the ground shake. And why are you wearing that fur on a hot day like this?"

The monkey did not answer the last question and looked very ashamed.

"I am sorry to disturb you," he said, "but I wanted to drink that cool water. I can't reach it and so I must spill it on the ground before I can drink it."

"Really, you ought to have more sense," said the lizard. "Just look at the ground." And he whisked round in a flash, so that one moment he was facing one way and the next he was facing the other. "It's all hot stone and dry dust," he went on. "If you spill the water then the ground will drink it all up before you could get a single drop. Think of something else and have the goodness to make less noise about it when other people are sleeping." And with that he darted under the pot once more.

The small brown monkey sat down on the stones of the desert and looked at the pot again, and felt thirstier than ever.

He had been sitting for a few minutes with the sun beating down on him, when suddenly he felt cold. He noticed that he was now sitting in shadow, and looking up he saw a great black shape hovering over him.

"Who's that?" asked the monkey.

"I am a monkey-eating eagle," said the big shape, coming nearer, "and who are you?"

Now the small brown monkey knew what was good for him, and fortunately he was clever enough to have an answer ready. "By a strange coincidence," he replied quickly, "I am an eagle-eating monkey, and I should be pleased to meet you."

The big bird hastily rose several feet higher into the blue sky.

"Have you by any chance," called the small brown monkey after him, "seen any water about in your travels?"

"From up here I can see everything," came the reply, "and the only water that I can see is the hippopotamus's pond." With that the great bird rose higher still. "Second on the left past the mango tree and first right after the paw-paw tree." And with that the great bird soared up and up until it disappeared in the sky.

It was a hot and thirsty little monkey who trudged back into the stuffy green heat of the jungle. He followed the direction given to him, and at last arrived at the hippopotamus's pond. But what a disappointment awaited him! Instead of cool, fresh water, as he had hoped, there was thick, steaming, muddy water.

"Ugh! I can't drink that!" said the sad creature, and he squatted down on his hind quarters and cried.

Now the hippopotamus had seen and heard all this from her position in the middle of the pool. But because she was almost completely under the water (all except her eyes and her nostrils) the monkey hadn't noticed her. At first she had kept quite still because she had been a little offended – I may as well admit it – by the monkey's unwillingness to drink her beautiful bathwater. However, she was a tender-hearted old thing and as soon as the monkey began to cry, she floated to the surface and, garlanded with smelly pond-weed, swam to the bank.

"There, there," she said comfortingly. "Did you want a drink, then?"

The monkey looked up quickly and gazed at the large smiling face which greeted him. In fact, he rather forgot his manners and *stared* at it, fascinated by the bristles on her chin. But he quickly remembered himself and said: "Good afternoon. Yes, I would very much like a drink, because I'm so hot and thirsty."

"Then just wait for me to climb out and I'll help you search through the jungle for water," said the hippopotamus.

It was such a well-meant and kind offer that the monkey felt he had to accept it, although he knew that apart from the water in the pot, which he couldn't reach, there wasn't a single drop in the whole jungle.

So he waited for the hippopotamus to come out of the pond and she did. And what do you think! The monkey noticed, with his eyes wide open with delight, that as she climbed out of the pond, the level of the water slowly went down.

"Oh, please get in again!" called the monkey excitedly.

"But I want to help you," insisted the hippopotamus.

"And so you will!" cried the small brown monkey.

With a puzzled look on her huge face, but nevertheless pleased to be useful, the hippopotamus sank slowly back into the water. Sure enough, as she did so the water rose again in the pond.

"Hurrah!" shouted the monkey, bounding away. Then remembering his manners again, he bounded back and said quietly: "Thank you very much for helping me. I am most grateful to you." And he ran off to the edge of the jungle.

Back at the pot he quickly collected an armful of big stones – the biggest he could find. He carried them to the side of the pot, climbed up on to the branch, and began to drop the stones in, ever so gently, one by one.

"Splash!" went the first one, faintly, as it hit the bottom.

"Splash!" went the next, a little louder.

And he dropped in more and more until the big pot was three-quarters filled with stones and – what do you think? – the water had risen to the very brim. All the monkey had to do then was to purse his lips and drink the fresh, cool water from the top of the pot.

"And when the water gets too low again," he said happily to himself, "I can always drop some more stones in."

It's a clever monkey who uses his eyes and his common sense.

*illustrated by Quentin Blake*

# SILLY SIMON

## *Mollie Clarke*

Once upon a time there was a very rich man who had a beautiful daughter. But the beautiful daughter could neither speak nor laugh.

The best doctors in all the land came to see the girl and they said, "This girl cannot speak because she cannot laugh. If someone can make her laugh then she will be able to speak."

The rich man said, "If any man can make my daughter laugh, I shall give him a bag of silver and a bag of gold."

After that, a hundred men had tried to make the rich man's daughter laugh, but not one of them had been able to do so.

Now in this land, there was a common and on the edge of the common was a little house and in the little house lived a poor woman and her son.

All day long the poor woman sat spinning but her son did nothing at all.

In the summer he sat in the sunshine doing nothing at all and in the winter he sat by the fire doing nothing at all.

Everyone called him Silly Simon.

At last the poor woman could stand it no longer. She said, "It is time you did some work. Away with you across the common and see if you can find something to do."

The next morning, Silly Simon set off across the common and very soon he met a farmer.

The farmer said, "I need a boy like you to drive the pigs. If you will drive the pigs I shall give you a penny."

So Silly Simon drove the farmer's pigs and at the end of the day the farmer gave him a bright, new penny.

Silly Simon held the penny in his hand and ran along home.

Silly Simon came to a stream and in the stream he saw silver fish and gold fish, but when he tried to catch a fish, his bright new penny slipped out of his hand and rolled into the stream.

When he got home, he told his mother what had happened.

"You stupid boy!" said his mother. "That is not the way to carry a penny. The way to carry a penny is to put it in your pocket and run along home. Now remember that!"

"Yes, I shall remember that," said Silly Simon.

On the second day, Silly Simon set off across the common and very soon he met a man with six cows.

The man said, "I need a boy like you to milk my cows. If you will milk my cows, I shall give you a jug of new milk." So Silly Simon milked the cows and at the end of the day the farmer gave him a jug of new milk.

Silly Simon said to himself, "Now what did my mother tell me? She said I was to put it in my pocket and run along home."

So he put the jug of milk in his pocket and he ran along home.

But when he got home his mother took the jug out of his pocket and there was not a drop of milk inside it. "You stupid boy!" said his mother. "That is not the way to carry a jug of milk. The way to carry a jug of milk is to hold it on your head and walk slowly home. Now remember that!"

"Yes, I shall remember that," said Silly Simon.

On the third day, Silly Simon set off across the common and very soon he met the farmer's wife.

The farmer's wife said, "I need a boy like you to feed my hens. If you will feed my hens, I shall give you a fresh cream cheese." So Silly Simon fed the hens and at the end of the day the farmer's wife gave him a fresh cream cheese. Silly Simon said to himself, "Now what did my mother tell me? She said I was to carry it on my head and walk slowly home."

So he put the fresh cream cheese on his head and walked home slowly in the sunshine.

But the cream cheese melted away in the hot sunshine and when his mother saw him, she said, "You stupid boy! That is not the way to carry a fresh cream cheese. The way to carry a fresh cream cheese is to hold it carefully in your hands and run along home. Now remember that!"

"Yes, I shall remember that," said Silly Simon.

On the fourth day, Silly Simon set off across the common and very soon he met a woodcutter.

The woodcutter said, "I need a boy like you to tie up my sticks.

If you will tie up my sticks, I shall give you a log of wood."

So Silly Simon tied up the sticks and at the end of the day, the woodcutter gave him a log of wood. Silly Simon said to himself, "Now what did my mother tell me? She said I was to hold it carefully in my hands and run along home."

So he held the log in his hands and tried to run home, but the log was too heavy and he had to leave it at the side of the road.

When his mother heard about this, she said, "You stupid boy! That is not the way to carry a log of wood. The way to carry a log of wood is to tie it with rope and pull it along home. Now remember that!"

"Yes, I shall remember that," said Silly Simon.

On the fifth day, Silly Simon set off across the common and very soon he met a butcher.

The butcher said, "I need a boy like you to sweep my floor. If you will sweep my floor, I shall give you a leg of mutton." So Silly Simon swept the floor and at the end of the day, the butcher gave him a leg of mutton. Silly Simon said to himself, "Now what did my mother tell me? She said I was to tie it with rope and pull it along home."

So he tied the leg of mutton with rope, put it on the ground and pulled it along home.

Now when his mother saw the leg of mutton all covered with dirt and dust, she said, "I do believe you are the stupidest boy in all the world. That is not the way to carry a leg of mutton.

The way to carry a leg of mutton is to lift it on to your shoulder and come along home. Now remember that!"

"Yes, I shall remember that," said Silly Simon.

On the sixth day, Silly Simon set off across the common and very soon he met a man with four donkeys.

The man said, "I need a boy like you to clean the stables. If you will clean the stables, I shall give you a donkey." So Silly Simon cleaned the stables and at the end of the day, the man gave him a donkey. Silly Simon said to himself, "Now what did my mother tell me? She said I was to lift it on to my shoulder and come along home."

So he lifted the great donkey on to his shoulder and set off for home.

Just then the rich man and his beautiful daughter passed by. When the beautiful daughter saw little Silly Simon carrying the great donkey on his shoulder, she began to laugh.

Then she said to her father, "Just look at that silly boy carrying a great donkey!"

The rich man said to Silly Simon, "You are the cleverest boy in the land because you have made my daughter laugh and speak. Here is a bag of silver and here is a bag of gold."

Silly Simon held the bag of gold in his right hand and the bag of silver in his left hand and ran along home as fast as he could run.

When his mother saw the silver and gold she said, "That is the way to carry bags of silver and gold. I always knew you were the cleverest boy in all the world."

*illustrated by Priscilla Lamont*

# THE EMPEROR'S OBLONG PANCAKE
## *Peter Hughes*

L ONG, long ago in the East there was an Emperor who loved pancakes. Every day of the year he had six pancakes for breakfast; great, big yellow ones they were, and a little bit brown on top; in fact, just done to a turn.

And, of course, they were round; as round as round as round.

One fine morning in spring, when all the almond trees in the palace courtyard were bursting into blossom, the Emperor came down to breakfast feeling especially merry. You see, it was his birthday.

"Happy birthday, Your Excellency," said the first footman, as the Emperor sat down at the breakfast table, and he pushed the Emperor's chair up snug behind his knees.

"Happy birthday, Your Excellency," said the second footman, as he laid out the Emperor's golden spoon, fork and knife in front of him.

"Happy birthday, Your Excellency," said the third footman, helping to tuck the Emperor's gleaming white napkin into his red velvet collar, and spreading it neatly over his gold-embroidered waistcoat.

"Happy birthday, Your Excellency," said the Court Chamberlain as he bowed low. Then he beckoned forward the first footman again, bearing a huge golden bowl full of hot, steaming porridge.

"And the same to you," said the Emperor, merrily, as he shook the sugar and poured the cream; and with that he set briskly to work, opening all his birthday cards with his left hand, and scooping porridge into his mouth with his right, as merry as merry could be.

In no time at all the Emperor's porridge was finished, and all his birthday cards were propped up in front of him. Immediately the third footman whisked away the empty plate, and the Court Chamberlain marched solemnly to the door, where he took up the big gong stick, made of solid ebony, and beat the big gong, made of solid brass. This was the signal for the fourth and fifth footmen to bring in the main dish.

At the far end of the dining-room the big bronze doors flew open, and in came the fourth and fifth footmen, bearing between them a broad silver dish with a broad silver dish-cover. Up the length of the dining-room they marched, with the Court Chamberlain walking in front, carrying his wand of office, until they reached the Emperor.

The fourth and fifth footmen bowed as low as low. "Happy birthday, Your Excellency," they cried together.

"And the same to you," beamed the Emperor, still as merry as ever, and he rubbed his hands together in anticipation, as the fourth and fifth footmen took the cover off the silver dish.

"Pancakes!" cried the Emperor. "How very nice! Capital!" just as if he didn't have pancakes every day of the year.

Then the fourth and fifth footmen, armed with huge silver forks, began carefully lifting the pancakes from the silver dish, one by one, and laying them on the Emperor's golden plate. Pale yellow, they were, and slightly, ever so slightly brown on top; in fact, just done to a turn; and, of course, they were all as round as round as round.

Out they came, one, two, three, four, five, and each as round and crisp as could be.

And now, as the Emperor reached for the sugar, out came the last pancake. Clang went the silver cover on the silver dish, and the Emperor was just about to dig in, when he stopped.

He stopped and he stared! He stopped and he stared and he gasped!

Then, trembling with fury, he rose slowly to his feet. His face began to turn bright purple, and he tore his white dinner napkin out of his red velvet collar and flung it across the room. Then he opened his mouth and roared.

And what he roared was: "OBLONG!"

Everybody stared in horror, and everybody trembled in fear. Then the five footmen, terrified out of their wits, turned tail and fled through the great bronze doors, which clanged shut behind them.

The Court Chamberlain had half a mind to follow them; but then he remembered that before being Court Chamberlain, he had been the bravest corporal in the Emperor's army. So he stood his ground.

"Excellency," said the Court Chamberlain, bowing right down to the ground, and raising his eyebrows at the same time.

"Oblong!" roared the Emperor again; then he stabbed with his fork, plonk right into the middle of the sixth pancake, and raised it high in the air like a flag.

"It's an insult!" he shouted "This pancake is oblong!"

And so it was; as oblong as oblong as oblong.

The Chamberlain stared at the pancake and the Emperor stared at the Chamberlain.

"Explain!" he roared.

"I… I can't, Your Excellency," stammered the Chamberlain. "That is, not just at the moment. However, I'll find out about it immediately, immediately, Excellency," and with a somewhat hasty bow he hurried away down the long, marble dining-room and out through the bronze double doors.

Left to himself, the Emperor began to feel rather foolish, standing there holding his fork aloft with the oblong pancake dangling from it. Besides, the other five pancakes looked all right. They smelled very nice too, and after all it was his birthday, and he was still hungry.

"Drat the thing!" said the Emperor, and stepping smartly over to the window he hurled the offending pancake as far as he could. Out across the courtyard it flew, and stuck in the top of one of

167

the almond trees, sending a shower of pale pink almond blossoms whirling down on to the marble pavement.

By and by the Emperor finished the five round pancakes, and he was just having an extra piece of toast to make up for the one pancake he hadn't had, when the bronze double doors flew open and the Court Chamberlain hurried in.

He was relieved to find the Emperor looking fairly calm again, and advancing up the long carpet, he bowed low.

"Excellency," he began.

"Well," said the Emperor, rather indistinctly through the toast.

"Excellency, it would appear it was a birthday present."

"A what?" asked the Emperor, a good deal surprised.

"Well, actually, Excellency, and in point of fact," said the Chamberlain, bowing till his forehead touched his shoes, "it was the frying pan."

The Emperor began to smile. "I think I see," he said. "The frying pan was a birthday present, and being oblong, it fried an oblong pancake."

The Court Chamberlain straightened up sharply. "Your Excellency's perspicacity is indeed remarkable," he said.

"Oh, I don't know," said the Emperor modestly, and in fact he didn't, but it sounded complimentary, and he was pleased to have guessed right.

He walked slowly back to his chair, and sat musing a while, twiddling the sugar spoon.

"You know," he said, slowly, "I rather like the idea. An oblong frying pan, eh? Oblong pancakes, what? Yes, I certainly like the idea. After all," he added, "one likes to be a little different, doesn't one?"

The Court Chamberlain was vastly relieved. "Of course, Excellency, exactly," he said. "Oh, yes indeed!"

"Good!" said the Emperor. "Then that's understood, oblong pancakes only in future." And with that he bounced away out of the dining-room, as merry as ever, to see to the day's business.

Now that, you might think, was the end of the story. So, indeed, it would have been if this had been an ordinary Emperor; but he wasn't; and he soon made up his mind that everyone in the Empire should share his great discovery. In no time at all the whole population was buying oblong frying pans and frying oblong pancakes; and those who were too poor to buy new ones took hammers or stones or lumps of wood and banged their round frying pans oblong. The Emperor had ordered it, and that was that.

As for the Emperor, he was still as merry as ever, and very pleased with himself for having had such an original idea. For by this time he was quite persuaded he had thought the whole thing out himself. He was still as merry as ever, until one morning in autumn, when the leaves of the almond trees in the courtyard were beginning to turn brown.

On that particular morning the Emperor was just finishing his sixth pancake when an uneasy feeling came over him.

Oblong pancakes, undoubtedly, were the only thing for a man of sense; but something still seemed not quite as it should be. The Emperor pondered, staring at his empty plate; and as he stared he began to smile.

"Of course," he murmured, "why didn't I think of it before? Oblong pancakes need oblong plates. It's common sense." Springing to his feet, he strode across the marble dining-room and tugged the bell-pull.

Down in the butler's pantry the Court Chamberlain was just going to start his own oblong pancake when the bell jangled so hard it nearly fell off the wall. Dropping his fork with a clatter, the Chamberlain seized his wand of office and rushed up the marble stairs and through the bronze double doors into the Emperor's dining-room. There he bowed low before the Emperor.

"Excellency?" said the Chamberlain, rather out of breath.

"Oblong pancakes need oblong plates," said the Emperor, briefly. "Arrange it."

"Excellency," said the Court Chamberlain, bowing again. And by breakfast-time the next morning, there before the Emperor was a fine golden plate, all new and gleaming, with the imperial arms stamped in the middle. Of course it was oblong.

The Emperor said nothing, but he was pleased all the same. He liked to have his orders promptly obeyed, and besides, one did like to be just a little different.

Of course the Emperor didn't stay different very long, because he soon had every potter and tinsmith in the Empire turning out oblong plates for every man, woman and child in the land. He was so proud of his good idea and besides he was not a selfish man.

But by the end of a week the Emperor was worrying again. He had a tidy mind, and it bothered him to see oblong plates on the table mixed up with cups and saucers which were round. They

170

didn't match. So – you've guessed it – the necessary orders were given, and in no time at all oblong cups and saucers were the rule throughout the country.

By this time the whole idea was beginning to become an obsession. Once started, the Emperor found himself unable to stop, and soon he was ordering something round to be changed to oblong every day.

As for the people, they knew what the Emperor was like when he got hold of an idea, and they soon began to guess what he would change next. Without waiting to be told, they began to throw out everything in their houses which was round, and to have everything oblong instead.

They had oblong saucepans, and oblong spoons and oblong bottles and oblong dishes. They ate oblong pies and oblong tarts and oblong cheeses. They wore oblong hats and they carried oblong umbrellas when it rained. They even bumped about the streets in carriages with oblong wheels. Oh, it was most uncomfortable, but the Emperor was bound to order it sooner or later, and he liked things done so fast, it was best to be prepared.

The Emperor soon learned how the people were so loyal that they tried to anticipate his every wish. But at the same time he couldn't help trying to think of new things to change before they did; and before long he began to order really difficult things like oblong apples and oblong eggs. He was the Emperor, of course, and however difficult it might be, his orders must be obeyed. All the farmers and gardeners and all the scientists and professors set to work to see that they were… and by the next autumn all the apple trees were loaded with oblong apples, and all the pear trees with oblong pears; and all the hens in the land, poor things, were laying oblong eggs like anything. Even the almonds on the almond trees in the palace courtyard were

oblong, and as the Emperor surveyed the scene from his dining-room window, he was filled with pride by his own quick thinking and the cleverness of his subjects.

What other monarch, he mused, could have achieved so much in so short a time? He stood there at the window, his hands clasped behind his back, puffing out his chest and surveying the scene with great satisfaction.

Among the oblong almonds the blue and green parakeets flitted and chattered; the fountains splashed gently in their oblong pools; ranged along the far side of the courtyard stood the

Emperor's great brass cannons, each with its pile of oblong cannonballs, and over all shone the soft, warm radiance of the autumn sun.

"What a beautiful day," sighed the Emperor contentedly, gazing up at the cloudless blue sky. "What a beautiful, beautiful d…"

*And then he stopped.*

*He stopped and he stared.*

*He stopped and he stared and he gasped.*

*Then he opened his mouth and roared.*

*And what he roared was: "ROUND!"*

The Court Chamberlain was just putting all the knives and forks and oblong spoons into the silver box marked 'Cutlery' when the Emperor roared "ROUND!" and the clatter was dreadful as they flew in all directions over the marble floor.

Pulling himself together, the Court Chamberlain bent low, raising his eyebrows at the same time.

"Excellency?"

"ROUND!" roared the Emperor again. "The sun is round! Have it changed at once!"

"The sun, Excellency?" stammered the Chamberlain, unable to believe his ears.

"Yes, you fool, the sun!" bellowed the Emperor, fairly dancing with rage. "That ugly, great, yellow, round thing hanging over my lovely oblong empire. It's ruining everything. Change it!"

The Court Chamberlain didn't dare to argue. He knew what the

Emperor was like when his mind was made up. So, although he hadn't the slightest idea what he was going to do, "Yes, Excellency," he said, and he bolted through the bronze double doors.

Once outside, the Chamberlain stopped, pulled out a large red spotted handkerchief and, leaning against a pillar, mopped his brow.

The sun! How in the name of all that was round could anybody make the sun oblong? It was too far away for one thing, and for another it was much too hot.

The Court Chamberlain opened the bronze doors a crack and peeped through. There was the Emperor, still fuming up and down in front of the window, and glaring up at the sun every few seconds, obviously expecting it to turn oblong any moment.

The Chamberlain shut the door, shrugged his shoulders hopelessly, and went off to try.

First he told all the Emperor's woodmen to chop down every tree in the Empire, and then he told all the Emperor's soldiers to build them up into a tall, tall tower, just outside the palace walls.

Every day the tower grew taller, and every day the Chamberlain climbed to the top to see if they were getting anywhere near the sun yet.

By and by there were no more trees left, and the sun seemed as far as ever, so they gave that up.

Then the Chamberlain asked all the Emperor's soldiers

if any of them would volunteer to be tied to one of the Emperor's oblong cannonballs and be shot up to the sun with a hammer in his hand. At first none of them would, but at last one of the very bravest said he would try. So they tied him firmly by the middle to an oblong cannonball, and put a heavy hammer in his hand. The Chamberlain told him exactly what to do when he reached the sun, and then they shut their eyes and shot him off.

Up he went like a rocket, but as he was rather fat he didn't go nearly high enough, and he soon came down again and stuck in the top of one of the almond trees in the courtyard; and then he fell out of the tree and splash into one of the oblong fountain pools. A very sorry sight he looked by the time the rest of them hauled him out. Still, they gave him a medal for trying, and the Chamberlain thought again.

He was just working out a method of throwing a stone into the sky without letting go of it, when finally the Emperor lost patience.

He rang all the bells in the palace very loudly, and the Chamberlain and the five footmen and the soldiers, and all the lords and ladies of the court besides, not to mention the people, hurried into the palace courtyard. The Emperor addressed them from the balcony.

"You are the most useless lot of subjects an Emperor ever had," he said crossly. "You don't deserve a progressive monarch like myself. I gave orders three weeks ago for the sun to be made oblong, and look at it – still as round as round as round – horrible!" and the Emperor shuddered.

"We have done our best, Excellency," ventured the Court Chamberlain.

"We've tried and tried and tried," cried all the Emperor's soldiers and the five footmen. All the lords and ladies nodded in agreement, though what they had done goodness only knew.

"Your best is not good enough," said the Emperor, crossly. "You all deserve to be boiled in oil. Instead, however…" he paused and surveyed them disdainfully… "Instead, however, I shall do the job myself."

"Do you not know," he went on, "that every evening the sun comes down to the edge of the earth? That is the time to deal with it." Then turning to the Court Chamberlain, he said, "Bring out my chariot."

The Chamberlain gave a signal, and the Sergeant-of-Horse led out the chariot, with four black horses dancing and prancing and kicking up the dust, and the Emperor climbed aboard.

They handed him a large packet of dried dates and a parcel of ready cooked pancakes for the journey, and also a pair of blacksmith's tongs and a heavy hammer, which the Emperor stowed under the seat.

Then, pressing his crown firmly on his head, he whipped up the horses, and shot away in a huge cloud of dust.

The people watched the dust cloud grow smaller in the distance until it dwindled out of sight. Then they all went home.

The next morning everyone was up early to see the sunrise. As the first pink glow appeared in the East, all the domes of the palace, and all the roofs in the town were crowded with onlookers. The pink turned to orange, and then to bright yellow, and all the people craned their necks and held their breath.

Then, suddenly, up popped the sun – and all the people groaned. It was still as round as round.

"It must be further than we thought," said the Chamberlain. "No wonder we never reached it with the tower. Still, the Emperor is so determined, he is sure to get there in the end. We shall have to be patient and wait."

So they did. But while they waited, the days grew into weeks and the weeks grew to months, and still the sun came up every morning as round as ever.

Meanwhile, however, some of the people, less patient than the others, began to get tired of bumping about in carriages and carts with oblong wheels. It was really very inconvenient; and so, one by one, they began to change all their oblong wheels back to round ones again. However, they all knew that what they had done was against the Emperor's wishes, so they all pretended not to notice what had happened.

And then, one day, quite suddenly, very much to everyone's surprise, and his own as well, the Emperor came back.

"Well I never!" said the Emperor, climbing stiffly out of his chariot. Everybody stared, and said "Well I never!" too.

"I must have taken a wrong turning somewhere," went on the

Emperor, feeling rather foolish. "How very, very annoying!"

So the Chamberlain arranged for the Emperor to have a wash and brush up and a little something to keep out the cold; and they stocked up the chariot again with food for the journey. Then, amid the cheers of all the people, the Emperor drove away to the West once more, and vanished over the horizon.

Again the days passed, and the weeks as well, but still the sun was as round as round; and not only the sun. I am afraid the people started to change other things besides the carriage wheels. It was a great strain on all the hens to keep laying oblong eggs, so they were allowed to go back to laying round ones; and of course that meant changing back all the egg cups as well. They were beginning to change the egg spoons too, when the Emperor suddenly came back again.

"Oh, bother!" said the Emperor, jumping crossly from his chariot. "I seem to have gone wrong again." But he was very determined, as you know by now, and he wouldn't give up. However, just to see what happened, this time he pointed his chariot the other way, and galloped rapidly away towards the East.

Immediately everyone went back to changing the spoons, and because the gardeners had forgotten to use the special fertilizer, all the fruit trees began to produce ordinary, round apples and oranges and pears and almonds once more.

And so it went on for a long while. The sun stayed as round as round, and gradually everything in the Empire which had once been oblong was changed to being round too. Every now and then the Emperor would suddenly arrive back again, and say "Oh, bother!" and gallop off in a new direction.

But as time passed it became clear that no matter in which direction he galloped, he always came back again to where he had started from. No one could understand it.

Then one day in spring, when the almond trees in the palace courtyard were bursting into blossom, the Emperor came back for the umpteenth time; but this time he didn't say, "Oh, bother!" Instead he came galloping up as merry as could be, and bounced out of his chariot and up the marble staircase into the palace.

Then he rang all the bells, and summoned the people into the courtyard.

Soon they were assembled, but they held their hats behind their backs, because, of course, they were all round, and they didn't want the Emperor to see. The Sergeant of the Guard had sentries stationed in front of the cannons, so as to hide the piles of round cannon balls from the Emperor.

The Emperor, looking very pleased with himself, stepped out on to the balcony, and addressed them.

"My people," he began, "you have been very patient. I have been away a long time, and you have remained loyal and obedient subjects in every way. I am very pleased with you all."

At this the people cheered, but they felt a little nervous, and no one more so than the Chamberlain. He could not help remembering all the things which had been changed from oblong to round against the Emperor's wishes.

But the Emperor was speaking again.

"My people," he said, "I have failed to reach the sun; but…" and he began to smile broadly, and puffed out his chest till all his decorations rattled and the buttons nearly flew off his waistcoat. "It no longer matters. Changing the sun is a very minor matter, after all, compared with the remarkable discovery I have made. My people," said the Emperor, proudly, "my dear people, your Emperor has established by personal experiment, and beyond all reasonable doubt, a new and amazing scientific fact. The world, in short… THE WORLD IS ROUND!"

You should have heard the cheering. The people cheered, and the soldiers cheered, the footmen cheered, the lords and ladies cheered; and none cheered louder than the Chamberlain.

The Emperor bowed and smiled, and smiled and bowed, and then he held his hand up again.

"The world is round, my people, as round as round as round. And very nice, too. So now, in consequence, it is my wish that everything in the Empire should be round as well – to match." The Court Chamberlain stepped forward and bowed as low as low: "Your Excellency," he said, "may it please Your Excellency, it is already done."

The Emperor was so pleased at this that he danced a little jig, clapping his hands and crying, "Capital, capital, capital!"

Then the Emperor turned and entered the marble dining room, followed by the Chamberlain and the five footmen.

"Now," said the Emperor, rubbing his hands, "what about breakfast?"

"May I suggest pancakes, Your Excellency?" ventured the Court Chamberlain with a smile.

"Excellent!" said the Emperor. "Nothing could be nicer."

"Would Your Excellency prefer them round or – or – oblong?" inquired the Chamberlain, bowing as low as low.

The Emperor thought for a moment, rubbing his chin, and then his eyes twinkled, and he said: "Oblong, please. I shall continue to have my pancakes oblong. After all, the frying pan was a birthday present, and I wouldn't like to hurt anyone's feelings. And besides," finished the Emperor, settling comfortably in his chair, "besides, one does like to be a little different, after all!"

*illustrated by Wendy Smith*

# THE LITTLE GIRL AND THE TINY DOLL
## *Aingelda Ardizzone*

THERE was once a tiny doll who belonged to a girl who did not care for dolls.

For a long time she lay forgotten in a mackintosh pocket until one rainy day when the girl was out shopping.

The girl was following her mother round a grocer's shop when she put her hand in her pocket and felt something hard.

She took it out and saw it was the doll. "Ugly old thing," she said and quickly put it back again, as she thought, into her pocket.

But, in fact, since she didn't want the doll, she dropped it unnoticed into the deep freeze among the frozen peas.

The tiny doll lay quite still for a long time, wondering what was to become of her. She felt so sad, partly because she did not like being called ugly and partly because she was lost.

It was very cold in the deep freeze and the tiny doll began to feel rather stiff, so she decided to walk about and have a good look at the place. The floor was crisp and white, just like frost on a winter's morning. There were many packets of peas piled one on top of the other. They seemed to her like great big buildings. The cracks between the piles were rather like narrow streets.

She walked one way and then the other, passing, not only packets of peas, but packets of sliced beans, spinach, broccoli and mixed vegetables. Then she turned a corner and found herself among beef rissoles and fish fingers. However, she did not stop but went on exploring until she came to boxes of strawberries; and then ice-cream.

The strawberries reminded her of the time when she was lost once before among the strawberry plants in a garden. Then she sat all day in the sun smelling and eating strawberries.

Now she made herself as comfortable as possible among the boxes.

The only trouble was that people were continually taking boxes out to buy them and the shop people were always putting in new ones.

At times it was very frightening. Once she was nearly squashed by a box of fish fingers.

The tiny doll had no idea how long she spent in the deep freeze. Sometimes it seemed very quiet. This, she supposed, was when the shop was closed for the night.

She could not keep count of the days.

One day when she was busy eating ice-cream out of a packet, she suddenly looked up and saw a little girl she had never seen before. The little girl was sorry for the tiny doll and wished she could take her home.

The doll looked so cold and lonely, but the girl did not dare to pick her up because she had been told not to touch things in the shop. However, she felt she must do something to help the doll and as soon as she got home she set to work to make her some warm clothes.

First of all, she made her a warm bonnet out of a piece of red flannel.

This was a nice and easy thing to start with.

After tea that day she asked her mother to help her cut out a coat from a piece of blue velvet.

She stitched away so hard that she had just time to finish it before she went to bed. It was very beautiful.

The next day her mother said they were going shopping, so the little girl put the coat and bonnet in an empty matchbox and tied it into a neat parcel with brown-paper and string.

She held the parcel tightly in her hand as she walked along the street.

As soon as she reached the shop she ran straight to the deep freeze to look for the tiny doll.

At first she could not see her anywhere. Then, suddenly, she saw her, right at the back, playing with the peas. The tiny doll was throwing them into the air and hitting them with an ice-cream spoon.

The little girl threw in the parcel and the doll at once started to untie it. She looked very pleased when she saw what was inside.

She tried on the coat, and it fitted. She tried on the bonnet and it fitted too.

She jumped up and down with excitement and waved to the little girl to say thank you.

She felt so much better in warm clothes and it made her feel happy to think that somebody cared for her.

Then she had an idea. She made the matchbox into a bed and pretended that the brown paper was a great big blanket. With the string she wove a mat to go beside the bed.

At last she settled down in the matchbox, wrapped herself in the brown-paper blanket and went to sleep.

She had a long, long sleep because she was very tired and, when she woke up, she found that the little girl had been back again and had left another parcel. This time it contained a yellow scarf.

Now the little girl came back to the shop every day and each time she brought something new for the tiny doll. She made her a sweater, a petticoat, knickers with tiny frills, and gave her a little bit of a looking-glass to see herself in.

She also gave her some red tights which belonged to one of her own dolls to see if they would fit. They fitted perfectly.

At last the tiny doll was beautifully dressed and looked quite cheerful, but still nobody except the little girl ever noticed her.

"Couldn't we ask someone about the doll?" the little girl asked her mother. "I would love to take her home to play with."

The mother said she would ask the lady at the cash desk when they went to pay for their shopping.

"Do you know about the doll in the deep freeze?"

"No indeed," the lady replied. "There are no dolls in this shop."

"Oh yes there are," said the little girl and her mother, both at once. So the lady from the cash desk, the little girl and her mother all marched off to have a look. And there, sure enough, was the tiny doll down among the frozen peas.

"It's not much of a life for a doll in there," said the shop lady, picking up the doll and giving it to the little girl. "You had better take her home where she will be out of mischief."

Having said this, she marched back to her desk with rather a haughty expression.

The little girl took the tiny doll home, where she lived for many happy years in a beautiful dolls' house. The little girl played with her a great deal, but best of all the tiny doll liked the company of the other dolls. They all loved to listen to her adventures in the deep freeze.

*illustrated by Posy Simmonds*

# Tomkin and the Three Legged Stool
## *Vivian French*

THERE was once a little tailor called Tomkin. He had no mother, no father, no brothers and no sisters. He had nothing that belonged to him except for his needles, his reels of cotton, his scissors and a three legged stool, but he sang and he whistled as he worked.

One night Tomkin had a dream. He dreamed that instead of eating hard bread and water for his supper he had hot cabbage soup with soft white rolls. He dreamed that instead of sleeping on a cold and draughty bench he had a warm and cosy bed with thick red blankets. He dreamed that instead of sitting all day on a little wooden stool with three legs he sat on a golden throne…

Tomkin sat up on his bench and rubbed his eyes.

"Well!" he said. "That was a good dream – the best I've ever had. Hot cabbage soup! Thick red blankets! And me a king – whatever can it mean?" He scratched his head, and looked at his three legged stool.

"What do you think?" he asked.

The three legged stool turned around twice and bowed.

"I think Your Majesty should go out and find your kingdom," it said.

"You're quite right," said Tomkin. "All I do here is mend shirts and stockings and sew on the mayor's buttons twice a week. I'll be off right away." He hopped off the bench and packed a bag with all his needles, three reels of cotton and a pair of sharp scissors.

"Now I'm ready," he said, but he didn't go out through the door.

"What are you waiting for?" asked the three legged stool.

"I was wondering if I'd be lonely, travelling all the way to my kingdom on my own," said Tomkin.

"It might be near, or it might be far," said the three legged stool. "Shall I come with you?"

"Yes, please," said Tomkin, "and when I'm king I promise I'll make you prime minister."

The stool spun round on one leg and sang:

*"Promises promises, one, two, three,*
*A king will never remember me."*

"Oh, yes, I will," said Tomkin, and they went through the door together.

Tomkin walked along the road with a hop, a skip and a jump, and the three legged stool trundled along beside him.

They walked through a forest and over a hill and down into the valley on the other side. Sometimes they talked, and sometimes they were silent, and sometimes Tomkin whistled a tune and the stool danced on its three wooden legs.

Down in the valley was a wide river and Tomkin and the three legged stool came to a stop.

"Oh, dear," said Tomkin, "I can't swim! Do you think my kingdom is on this side or the other side of the river?"

"It might be far, or it might be near," said the stool. "But as to swimming – just throw me in and hold on tightly!"

Tomkin waded into the rushing water, holding on to the stool. The current caught him and swirled him off his feet, but the wooden stool bobbed and floated on top of the water.

"*Oof!*" spluttered Tomkin, and he kicked and splashed until he and the stool were on the far side of the river. They staggered up the bank, and sat down to rest.

"You're a very good swimmer," Tomkin said to the three legged stool. "And when I'm king I promise I'll make you prime minister."

The stool spun round on two legs and sang:

*"Promises promises, one, two, three,
A king will never remember me."*

"Yes, I will," said Tomkin indignantly.

Tomkin and the stool walked on and on, and as they walked they noticed that the grass and bushes on either side of the path were dusty brown. The trees had no leaves and the earth was hard and cracked.

"It looks as if it hasn't rained here for ages and ages," said Tomkin. "But it must be going to rain soon – look at the sky!"

The sky was leaden grey, and a huge black cloud was swirling round the top of the hill ahead of them. They could see a village half-way up the hill, and beyond the village was a castle.

"Maybe that's my kingdom," Tomkin said.

"Maybe it is," said the stool. "It certainly looks as if all the people have come out to meet us."

Tomkin stopped and stared. The three legged stool was quite right – many men and women and children were hurrying down the hill towards them.

Tomkin shook his head. "I don't think I want to be king here," he said. "All these people look as sad as sad can be."

A bony little girl reached Tomkin and the three legged stool first.

"Oh, please!" she gasped, clutching at Tomkin's arm. "Please – have you come to make it rain?"

"What?" Tomkin said. "What do you mean? There's the biggest blackest cloud I ever saw over there – it must be about to rain puddles and ponds and lakes and seas any moment now."

The little girl began to sob and to cry, although not one tear came out of her eyes.

"But that's just it!" she wailed. "The cloud is always there – but it never, ever rains! All our rivers have dried up, and we've had no water now for days and weeks and months. Our cows and sheep have run away, and we have nothing left to eat but one cupful of flour. All our fields are dry and bare except for one small cabbage. And if it doesn't rain soon, we will all dry up into dust and blow away in the wind."

Tomkin looked around him at all the people. They were gazing at him, their eyes huge and hopeful in their thin pinched faces. He looked up at the black cloud, and he shifted his bag on his back and rubbed his nose.

"Well…" he said.

"Ahem," said the three legged stool in a small voice beside him. "Doesn't that cloud look full of rain? As full of rain as a bag might be full of needles and reels of cotton… but one snip from your scissors and they'd all fall out!"

"*Oh!*" said Tomkin. "Oh, yes! How clever you are – when I'm king I'm certainly going to make you prime minister!"

The stool spun round on three legs and sang:

*"Promises promises, one, two, three,
A king will never remember me."*

"Just you wait and see!" said Tomkin, and he marched on along the path and up the hill.

"Be careful!" the stool called after him. "A little can go a very long way!"

"I know what I'm doing," said Tomkin.

Up and up he went; past the village and past the castle until he was at the top of the hill and the huge black cloud was billowing just above his head. Tomkin swung the bag off his back and pulled out his scissors.

"Look at me!" he shouted.

*Snip! Snap! Rip!* Tomkin cut three long slashes right across the cloud. WHOOSH! the rush of rain washed him off his feet and sent him gasping and tumbling all the way back down to the bottom of the hill.

"HURRAH! HURRAH! HURRAH!" shouted the men and the women and the children, and they danced round and round in the silver sheets of pouring rain. They laughed and they sang and they cried and they cheered, and they picked up Tomkin and carried him back up the hill to the castle.

"You must be our king!" they said, and they sat him on a golden throne and put a golden crown on his head. They fetched him hot cabbage soup and soft white rolls, and they showed him his bed heaped with thick red blankets.

At the bottom of the hill the three legged stool stood and waited for Tomkin. It stood there with the rain beating down on it, and a cold wind blowing about it. In a small, sad voice it sang:

*"Promises promises, one, two, three,*
*When will the king remember me?"*

It went on raining. It rained without stopping, day and night, night and day. The trees and the fields grew green, and then became dark and heavy with the never-ending rain. Up in the castle Tomkin laughed and danced and sang, but as the rains went on he watched the rivers begin to flow again, and then fill and fill until they flooded their banks and rushed and gushed all over the countryside. The men and the women and the children stopped being happy and began to complain.

"What's the use of rain if it never stops?" they asked each other. "We were unhappy before, but if the floods wash our village away we'll be even worse off." And they walked up the path to the castle and demanded to see King Tomkin.

"You must stop the rain and bring back the sun," they said. "If you can't, we'll take away your crown and send you off on your travels again."

"Oh, dear," said Tomkin. "Well – maybe I could sew the holes together." He put his bag on his back and walked out of the castle and up to the top of the hill with the villagers following behind him. The black cloud was still in the sky, but it had poured out so much water that it was now high up, and far beyond his reach. Tomkin rubbed his nose.

"I need a ladder," he said. "I need lots of ladders."

"Then will you make it stop raining?" asked a little boy.

Tomkin nodded. "I'll try," he said.

"Hurrah!" shouted the little boy. "King Tomkin is going to mend the cloud!"

All the men and women and children from the village went hurrying off through the rain to fetch their ladders. They fetched their tables, and they fetched their chairs, and they heaped them one on top of the other into a tower that rose higher and higher.

"It's not high enough," Tomkin said. "What else have you got?"

They brought out beds and baths and chests of drawers. They carried dressers and cupboards and baskets and buckets and boxes, and piled them up and up.

"Is there anything else?" asked Tomkin.

"Nothing," said the villagers, staring at the tottering tower and shaking their dripping heads. "There's not so much as a bead box left to bring."

"All right," said Tomkin. "Now I'll see what I can do." And he began to climb.

Up went Tomkin, pulling himself up the ladders and climbing up and over the cupboards and chairs. Soon he could see the world around him for miles and miles, and still he climbed up and up. The big black cloud grew closer and closer, and he shook the rain from his eyes and kept on climbing.

Tomkin reached the top of the tower. He stood on the highest chair and stretched upwards... and he couldn't reach. He could see the three long splits in the cloud, but he was just too far away to touch them.

"I can't do it!" Tomkin said. "I can't reach."

The villagers began to whisper to each other and to mutter and to growl.

"Throw down your crown, Tomkin!" they shouted. "You're no king of ours! Throw down your crown, and be on your way!"

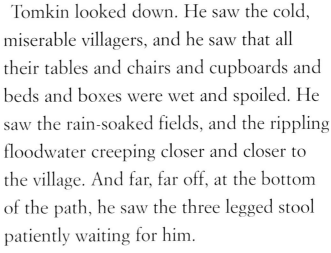

Tomkin looked down. He saw the cold, miserable villagers, and he saw that all their tables and chairs and cupboards and beds and boxes were wet and spoiled. He saw the rain-soaked fields, and the rippling floodwater creeping closer and closer to the village. And far, far off, at the bottom of the path, he saw the three legged stool patiently waiting for him.

Tomkin took a deep breath. "I cut the cloud too deeply and I've made it rain for ever and ever," he said. "And I forgot my oldest friend. I don't deserve to be a king," and he tossed the crown to the ground. His tears dropped down and mixed with the streams of water flowing down the hill… down to the three legged stool.

Up jumped the stool, and hurried up the hill.

"Stop!" it called. "Wait for me!" And it scurried through the groups of wailing villagers to the bottom of the tower.

Tomkin was sitting at the top with his head in his hands, but when he heard the stool calling he sat up straight and wiped his eyes.

Everyone watched the stool scrambling up the tower. Up and up it went, and when it reached the top Tomkin held it steady.

"I'm so sorry I forgot you," he said. "I really, truly am."

"No time for that now," said the stool as it balanced itself on top of the very topmost chair. "Come along – climb on me." Tomkin took his needles and thread out of his bag, and climbed on the stool. He was just high enough to reach the three long rips in the cloud and he began to sew.

He sewed all day long without stopping once, and gradually the rain grew less and less, until by the evening there was only a fine mist in the air.

"A couple more stitches and I'll be done," said Tomkin.

"That's good," said the stool.

Tomkin stopped suddenly.

"Oh!" he said. "Oh, no!"

"What's the matter?" asked the stool.

"It's no good," Tomkin said, "It's no good at all. There are needle holes in the cloud at the beginning and end of every stitch. I can see thousands of water drops squeezing through them – I'll *never* be able to stop the rain."

"Nobody wants you to stop the rain for ever," said the stool. "Finish your stitching."

"But it's no good," Tomkin said. "The whole village will be washed away, and it's all my fault." He made his last stitch and pulled it tight.

"Well done," said the stool. "Now look!"

Tomkin looked. The setting sun had come creeping out from behind the cloud and was shining through the mist. A rainbow was shimmering from one side of the hill to the other, and the puddles and ponds and lakes were shining golden mirrors of light.

"KING TOMKIN! KING TOMKIN!" called the villagers. "Come down and take up your crown!"

Tomkin shook his head, and began climbing down the tower with the three legged stool close behind him. Half-way down, a gust of wind blew a flurry of raindrops against Tomkin's face.

"Why!" he said. "The rain's like silver needles! It must be blowing through the needle holes in the cloud – but it isn't rushing and gushing like it was before."

"That's right," said the stool. "But a little can go a very long way."

Tomkin reached the ground, picked up the crown and handed it to the oldest villager.

"I'm not fit to be a king," he said, "but if you want someone wise and clever I think you should ask the three legged stool."

The villager bowed to the stool, and the stool bowed back.

"A king," said the stool, "should always know when he's made a mistake."

"Quite so," said the oldest villager.

"And a king should be willing to work all day without stopping for the good of his people," said the stool.

"My thoughts exactly," said the oldest villager.

"And a king should be as happy when he has nothing but a bag of needles as when he has a golden throne."

"I couldn't have put it better myself," said the oldest villager, and he picked up the golden crown and handed it back to Tomkin.

"Hurrah for King Tomkin!" shouted all the villagers.

Tomkin held up his hand and the men and the women and the children were silent.

"Thank you very much," he said, and he bowed. "But I will only be king if the three legged stool is prime minister."

"It will be my pleasure," said the three-legged stool.

"Hurrah for the three legged stool! Three cheers for our prime minister! And three more cheers for our wonderful king!" and the villagers picked Tomkin up and carried him off to the castle.

The three legged stool and the oldest villager walked up the path together.

"The best king of all," said the oldest villager, "is a king who keeps his promises."

And the stool sang:

*"Promises promises, one, two, three,*
*This is the king for you and me!"*

and he followed Tomkin into the castle with a hop, a skip and a jump.

*illustrated by James Mayhew*

# THE MOSSY ROCK

### *African folk tale, retold by Ruth Manning-Sanders*

ONE early morning, Anansi, the great big spider, the clever one, the cunning one, was in the forest looking for food, when he saw a rock with moss growing all over it, just like a thick green coat.

"Oh, oh!" says Anansi,

"*What a very curious stone*
  *All with green moss overgrown!*"

And no sooner had he said those words than he fell to the ground in a faint, because there was a strong spell on the rock.

He didn't come to himself till evening, and then he hurried home and went to bed, hungry, because he hadn't had anything to eat all day. He woke up next morning hungrier than ever; but he didn't mind – he had a fine plan in his head. So he went to call on Bush Goat.

"Good morning, Bush Goat. I'm off into the forest to look for food. Would you care to come with me? Four eyes are better than two, and we can share what we find."

Bush Goat thought that was a good idea, and they set off together.

In the forest Anansi said, "This looks a likely path." And he led the way to the mossy rock.

Bush Goat stared at the rock and said, "Just look!

"*What a very curious stone*
  *All with green moss overgrown!*"

And no sooner had Bush Goat said those words than he fell to the ground in a dead faint.

"Ha! ha!" laughed Anansi. "*You* won't wake up yet awhile, my friend! But it won't do to leave you lying here, lest you put two and two together when you *do* wake." So he dragged Bush Goat away, and laid him under a tree at some distance from the mossy rock. Then away he scampered to Bush Goat's house, ate up all Bush Goat's store of food, and carried off all he could lay his hands on of Bush Goat's little treasures.

Bush Goat woke up in the evening. He was very puzzled. "Dear me!" said he. "What am I doing here under this tree? I dreamed that I came out to look for food with Anansi, but I must have been wandering in my wits, since here I find myself alone! I do hope I'm not going to be ill! I must hurry home and take some medicine."

But when Bush Goat got home, and found his larder empty and all his little treasures stolen, why then poor Bush Goat sat down and shed tears. "I am a most unfortunate creature!" he cried. "A most unfortunate creature!"

But he never thought that Anansi had anything to do with his misfortune.

Next day, Anansi played the same trick on Stag, and the day after that on Antelope. He thought he had hit on a splendid way of living, getting food every day without having to work for it. On the fourth day he played the same trick on Bush Cow. But Bush Cow was so big and heavy that when she fell senseless, Anansi couldn't drag her away from in front of the stone.

What to do now? Anansi couldn't leave Bush Cow lying there to give the game away. So he hurried to fetch all his sister's children. And it was *heave ho*! and push and pull, till at last they got Bush Cow safely away, and lying in the forest at some distance from the mossy rock. Then they all went to Bush Cow's house and shared out what they found there. Anansi wasn't too pleased about this; he would rather have kept everything for himself; and he would have been less pleased had he known that his trick had been discovered. But he didn't know, and he couldn't know, that Spotted Deer had been strolling in the forest, and had seen all that had happened.

Next morning, when Anansi came out of his house, there was Spotted Deer.

"Good morning, Anansi!"

"Good morning, Spotted Deer! I'm just off into the forest to look for food. If you would care to come along with me, we can share what we find. Four eyes are better than two."

"Yes, I'll come with you, Anansi."

So off they went together. And when they came to the mossy rock, Anansi stood and stared.

Spotted Deer stood and stared.

Anansi said, "Spotted Deer, why don't you say something?"

Spotted Deer said, "What shall I say?"

Anansi said, "Well, isn't there something very curious here?"

Spotted Deer said, "Isn't there something very curious here?"

Anansi said, "Oh, you have no wits! Say it! Say it!"

Spotted Deer said, "Say what?"

Anansi said, "Don't you see? Something is growing on something!"

Spotted Deer said, "Don't you see? Something is growing on something!"

Anansi said, "I've no patience with you! Come on now, just say it!"

Spotted Deer said, "I've no patience with you – is that what you mean?"

"No, no!" shrieked Anansi. "Say 'What a very'... *you* know!"

"What a very… *you* know!" said Spotted Deer. "There, I've said it!"

"You haven't said it, you haven't said it!" screamed Anansi, dancing with rage. "You know what you ought to say – you're just being pig-headed!"

"I'm not being pig-headed," said Spotted Deer. "If you don't tell me what to say – how can I say it?"

"Then say," screamed Anansi, quite beside himself, "Say
*What a very curious stone*
*All with green moss overgrown!*"

Well, of course, as soon as Anansi said those words, he fell down in a faint.

But Spotted Deer didn't say anything. He just chuckled. He went away and left Anansi lying. He spent the day going round to all the other animals, and warning them about Anansi. So that when Anansi came to himself in the evening, there they all were, standing round and laughing at him. He crept home in a sulk, and very hungry.

And that was the end of his getting food and goods by trickery.

*illustrated by Diana Mayo*

# The Kingdom Under the Sea

*Japanese folk tale,*
*retold by Margaret Mayo*

ONE summer evening, long ago, a lad called Urashima Taro was walking across the beach after a day's fishing when he saw a turtle lying helpless on its back, slowly waving its flippers. So he bent down and picked it up.

"You poor creature," he said, "I wonder who turned you upside down and left you here to die in the sun? Some thoughtless young children who knew no better, I suppose."

He carried the turtle over the sands and waded out into the sea, as deep as he could, before lowering it into the water. And as he let it go, he called out, "Off you go, venerable turtle – and may you live for a thousand years!"

The next morning Urashima rowed out in his boat, as usual, throwing his fishing line as he went. When he had passed the other boats, and was a long way out at sea and all alone, he took a rest and let the boat drift on the waves.

It was then that he heard someone softly calling: "Urashima! Urashima Taro!"

He looked round, but there was not another boat in sight. Then he heard again: "Urashima! Urashima Taro!" It seemed to come from close by. So he looked again, and then he saw a turtle, swimming beside the boat.

"Turtle," he said, "was it you who called my name just now?"

"Yes, honourable fisherman, I was the one who spoke," answered the turtle. "Yesterday you saved my life, and today I have come to thank you and offer to take you to Ryn Jin, the palace of the Dragon King under the Sea, who is my father."

Urashima was astonished. "The Dragon King under the Sea is your father!" he said. "Surely not!"

"It is true. I am his daughter," she answered. "And if you climb on my back, I will take you to him."

Urashima thought that it would be a fine thing to see the kingdom under the sea, so he climbed out of the boat and sat himself down on the turtle's back.

Immediately they were off, skimming across the waves. And when it seemed they could go no faster, the turtle dived down into the depths of the sea. For a long time they sped through the water, passing whales and sharks, playful dolphins and shoals of silvery fish. At last Urashima saw in the distance a magnificent coral gate decorated with pearls and glittering gems, and beyond it the long sloping roofs and gables of a coral palace.

"We are approaching the gateway of my father's palace," said the turtle, and even as she spoke they reached it. "Now, from here, please, you must walk."

She turned to a swordfish who was the keeper of the gate and said, "This is an honoured guest from the land of Japan. Please show him the way to go." And with that she swam off.

And the swordfish led Urashima into an outer courtyard where a great company of fish, row upon row of octopus and cuttlefish, bonito and plaice, bowed graciously towards him.

"Welcome to Ryn Jin, the palace of the Dragon King under the Sea!" they chorused. "Welcome and thrice welcome!"

Then the great company of fish escorted Urashima through to an inner courtyard that led to the great door of the coral palace. The door opened and there stood a radiantly beautiful Princess. She wore flowing garments of red and green, shot through with all the colours of a wave with sunlight on it, and her long black hair streamed over her shoulders in the style of long ago.

"I welcome you to my father's kingdom," she said, "and ask you to stay here for a while in the land of everlasting youth, where summer never dies and sorrow never comes."

As Urashima listened to her words and gazed at her beautiful face, a feeling of contentment flooded over him. "My only wish is that I might stay here with you in this land for ever," he said.

"Then I shall be your bride and we shall live together always," said the Princess. "But first we must ask my father for his permission."

And the Princess took him by the hand and led him through long corridors to her father's great hall. There they knelt before the mighty lord, the Dragon King under the Sea, and bowed so low that their foreheads touched the floor.

"Honourable father," said the Princess, "this is the youth who saved my life in the land of men, and, if it pleases you, he is the one whom I have chosen to be my husband."

"It pleases me," the Dragon King answered, "but what does the fisher-lad say? Does he accept?"

"Oh... I gladly accept," said Urashima.

So then there was a wedding feast. And when the Princess and Urashima had pledged their love, three times three, with a wedding cup of saké wine, the entertainments began. Soft music was played, and strange and wonderful rainbow-coloured fish danced and sang.

The next day, when the celebrations were over, the Princess showed Urashima some of the marvels of her father's coral palace and his kingdom, and the greatest of these was the garden of the four seasons.

To the east lay the garden of spring, where the plum and cherry were in full blossom and birds of all kinds sang sweetly. To the south the trees were clothed in the green of summer and the crickets chirruped lazily. In the west the autumn maples were ablaze with flame-coloured leaves and the chrysanthemums bloomed. While in the north stood the winter garden where the bamboos and the earth were covered in snow, and the ponds were thick with ice.

Now there were so many things to see and wonder at in the kingdom under the sea that Urashima forgot about his own home and his old life. But after a few days, he remembered his parents.

He said to the Princess, "By now my mother and father must think that I have been drowned at sea. It must be three days or more since I left them. I must go, immediately, and tell them what

has happened."

"Wait," she said. "Wait a little longer. Stay at least one more day, here with me."

"It is my duty to go and see my parents," he answered. "But I will return to you."

"Then I must become a turtle again and carry you to the land above the waves," she said. "But, before you leave, accept this gift from me." And the Princess gave him a beautiful, three-tiered lacquer box, tied round with a red silk cord.

"Keep this box with you always, but do not open it, whatever happens."

And Urashima promised that he would not open the box.

Once again the Princess became a turtle, Urashima sat astride her back, and they were off. For a long time they rode through the sea, and then, at last, they soared upwards and reached the waves. Urashima turned his face towards the land and saw again the mountains and the bay he knew so well. They came to the beach, and he stepped ashore.

"Remember," said the turtle. "Do not open the box."

"I will remember," he said.

He walked across the sands and took the path that led to his home. But as he looked around, a strange fear came over him. The trees somehow looked different. So did the houses. And he didn't recognise anyone he saw. When he reached his own house, it too looked different. Only the little stream in the garden and a few stepping stones were the same.

He called: "Mother! Father!" And an old man whom he had never seen before opened the door.

"Who are you?" asked Urashima. "And where are my mother and father? And what has happened to our house? Everything has changed. And yet it is only three days, since I, Urashima Taro, lived here."

"This is my house," said the old man, "and it was my father's and my father's father's before him. But I have heard that a man called Urashima Taro once lived here. The story goes that one day he went fishing and didn't come back, and then, not long after, his old parents died of sorrow. But that was about three hundred years ago."

Urashima shook his head. It was hard to believe that his mother and father, and all his friends too, had died long, long ago. He thanked the old man and walked slowly back to the shore and sat down on the sands.

He felt sad. "Three hundred years," he thought. "Three hundred years must be only three days in the kingdom under the sea."

Now as he sat there, he held the lacquer box the Princess had given him in his hands, and his fingers idly played with the red silk cord. And the cord came undone. Without thinking what he was doing, he opened the first box. Three soft wisps of smoke came swirling out and curled around him; and the handsome youth became an old, old man.

He opened the second box. There was a mirror inside it; and he looked and he saw that his hair was grey and his face was old and wrinkled. He opened the third box. A crane's feather drifted out, brushed across his face and settled on his head; and the old man changed into a bird – a beautiful and elegant crane.

The crane flew up and looked out over the sea, and he saw a turtle, floating on the waves, close to the shore. The turtle looked up, and she saw the crane. And then she knew that her husband, Urashima Taro, would never ever return to her father's kingdom under the sea.

*illustrated by Peter Utton*

# JESSAME AND THE VERY FANCY DRESS
*Julia Jarman*

THERE was a Very Fancy Dress in the museum opposite Holly Bush House. It was a beautiful blue dress with a very tiny waist and a very sticking-out skirt with *paniers*. Grandpa said they were paniers. They were like big bows and they made the sticking-out skirt look even more sticking-out, and they made the tiny waist look even tinier. Grandpa said the Very Fancy Dress looked very uncomfortable, but Jessame said it was beautiful. It was the most beautiful dress she had ever seen.

There were lots of beautiful dresses in the museum including a duchess's wedding dress with silver lace, but it wasn't as beautiful as the Very Fancy Dress. Besides, as Jessame told Grandpa, the duchess's dress shouldn't really have been there. It was a grown-up's dress and the museum was a museum of childhood, wasn't it? The Bethnal Green Museum of Childhood was its proper name, and Jessame liked to give things their proper names. The museum was full of things belonging to children in days gone by. It was full of games and toys and clothes – just a few clothes – which children played with and wore long ago, and Jessame loved it.

She loved it so much she called it *her* museum – and Grandpa said it *was* her museum because it was everybody's museum. It belonged to the people. That's why it was free. It really was free. You could go in as often as you liked *without paying* and look at all the lovely things. Jessame went ever so often. She could see it from her bedroom window and if the day was grey when she woke up, and if she didn't have to go to school, she would say, "Let's go to my museum today, Grandpa Williams. Do you think that's a good idea?" And nearly always Grandpa would say, "Yes, Jessame Aduke. That's a very good idea."

Grandpa's friend, Mr Sanderson, was the doorman at the museum, and he always opened the door very grandly when he saw Jessame and Grandpa coming up the big circular drive. And he always looked very surprised when Jessame wouldn't go in! His mouth fell open and his eyebrows disappeared under his peaked cap – every time! Even though he knew that Jessame never went in straight away. She always carried on walking – or running sometimes – past the doorway and right round the other side of the big circular drive, and half way round again, till she reached the doorway again, and then she would go in.

And this time Grandpa would stand on one side of the entrance, and Mr Sanderson would stand on the other and Jessame would enter very grandly. Mr Sanderson would touch his peaked cap and say, "What would Miss Olusanya like to see first today?" And Jessame would stop and say, "The dolls' houses I think, and then the toy theatre with the button you press to change the scenery." Or sometimes she would say, "The motor cars and then the finger puppets, please." She always kept the Very Fancy Dress till last.

And Mr Sanderson would say, "I think you know the way, Madam, but if you need any assistance…"

But Jessame wouldn't be there. She didn't need any assistance.

She did know the way – straight ahead to the dolls' houses in their big glass cases, or up the stairs to the ride-on toys and the pretend shops, also in big glass cases. That was the only thing wrong with the museum, the big glass cases. How she longed to ride on the ride-ons or buy things from the pretend shops or play with all the tiny things inside the houses. She could never make up her mind which was her favourite house. She very much liked the one called Miss Miles's House because the notice said Miss Miles had made it *when a child, in the 1890s*. It was very grand. It had ten rooms filled with pretty furniture and on the floor of the parlour there was a tiny book, as if a small person had just stopped reading it and was coming back in a minute.

Jessame wondered how old Miss Miles had been when she'd made her house, and whether she'd made all the things to go in it.

Nuremberg House was very interesting too, and the most interesting thing in that was a baby-walker! It was just like the one Baby Mark had, like a pair of pants in the middle of a square frame with wheels. Mark sat in his and walked at the same time. But this one was over three hundred years old. It had been made in 1673! Grandma had been ever so surprised when Jessame had told her. In fact Jessame had to take her to see it, because Grandma had thought baby-walkers were a modern invention. She'd said, "Well I never," three times over when she saw it and, "Well now, there's nothing new under the sun is there?"

So Jessame always went to see the houses, and she nearly always went to see the magic lantern shows. There were lots of these, and when you pressed a button a picture lit up, and when you pressed the button again the picture changed. Jessame's favourite was of the zoo in Paris. One picture was of a lion in a cage, and when you pressed the button it jumped out of the cage! Then Jessame would run – not because she was frightened – but because she couldn't wait any longer. She ran up the stairs, round the balcony to the other side, to the glass cases with costumes – and there was the Very Fancy Dress.

Each time she saw it, it looked more beautiful and Jessame stood still and gazed at it. She pressed her nose against the glass and imagined herself as Cinderella going to the ball. She imagined herself riding in a carriage and dancing with the prince. Sometimes she imagined so hard that she wouldn't notice Grandpa standing beside her, till he said, "It's midnight, Cinderella. Time to go home before you turn into a pumpkin." And for a moment she would believe him. Then she would sigh and say, "Isn't it the fanciest dress you've ever seen, Grandpa Williams?" And Grandpa would chuckle.

But it *was* the fanciest dress she had ever seen, and it *was* her museum, so when one Friday at school Mrs Pearce said, "We are going to have a Fancy Dress Party, children," Jessame knew exactly what she would wear. Mrs Pearce went on to explain what she meant because some people didn't know what a Fancy Dress Party was. She said that it didn't mean just wearing your best clothes, your party clothes, it meant dressing up as somebody or something else. Jessame hardly listened. She didn't need to.

She told Grandma all about it as soon as they met at the school gate. "And I shall wear the Very Fancy Dress from my museum," she said.

And Grandma said, "Don't set your heart on it, Jessame. I don't think you can borrow dresses from museums." But Jessame said she thought she would be able to, just once.

She told Grandpa as soon as he got home from the telephone works and she told him that he must go to see Mr Sanderson the very next day and arrange to borrow the Very Fancy Dress, but even Grandpa shook his head. "I think that's 'Not Allowed', Jessame Aduke. You see, the dresses in the museum are very old and fragile. If people started wearing them they might fall to pieces."

Jessame said she wasn't people, she was just one person, and she made Grandpa promise that they would go the next day and ask Mr Sanderson. Grandpa said he would do better than that. He would ask the curator. She was the person in charge, but he still said he thought the answer would be 'no'.

When her mum came home, Jessame told her all about the Fancy Dress Party, and the Very Fancy Dress in the museum and how she wanted to wear it. Mrs Olusanya shook her head and said, "Don't set your heart on it, Jessame" – just like Grandma had, but she also said, "I think I'll come with you tomorrow, Jessame. I'd like to see that Very Fancy Dress. We can all ask the curator."

The curator said no. She was very sorry, but no. It was just not possible. If she let Jessame borrow the dress, she would have to let everybody borrow the dress and she couldn't.

Jessame was upset. Everybody tried to cheer her up. Grandma said, "Why not go as Mrs Tiggywinkle?"

Grandpa said, "Why not go as a parrot? Jacko would like that."

Jacko sat on Jessame's shoulder. He said, "Like that. Like that," and pecked her ear very gently.

But Jessame didn't want to go as anything else. She didn't want to go as a hedgehog or a parrot. She wanted to go as Cinderella in the Very Fancy Dress.

When she got to school on Monday the whole class were talking about their fancy dresses. They didn't sound a bit fancy to Jessame. Jason, the caretaker's son, was going as a beetle. His mum was making his costume out of dustbin bags. Jamila was going as a newspaper – wearing *newspapers*! The three McFigginses were going as turtles. Jessame didn't want to be a beetle or a newspaper or a turtle. She wanted to be Cinderella in the Very Fancy Dress.

When her mum came to kiss her goodnight, Jessame told her how sad she was. Mrs Olusanya said, "I'm sure you'll think of something else, Jessame." But Jessame said she wouldn't. There was only one fancy dress in her head, and while it was there, there wasn't room for anything else. So then her mum said, "Well let me think of something, Jessame. It will be a surprise. Just one thing, you must promise to try to like it a little bit. I don't want to try hard for nothing."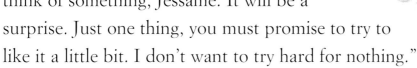

So Jessame promised, and hoped she would be able to *look* as if she liked whatever her mum decided on. She didn't want to hurt her mum's feelings.

The funny thing was, that soon after that, she did start to be a little bit interested. Two nights later when she lay in bed listening

to her mum's sewing machine whirring, she started to become curious, curious enough to get out of bed and get a drink of water, but when she got to the sitting-room door – and you had to go through the sitting-room to get to the kitchen – the door wouldn't open, and the whirring stopped.

"What is it, Jessame?" said her mum, who must have seen the door handle moving.

"I want a drink of water, please," said Jessame.

"Well, get it from the bathroom," said her mum.

"There isn't a cup in the bathroom," said Jessame, who didn't know whether there was or not.

"Well, go back to bed and someone will bring you one."

The someone was Grandpa.

"What's Mum making?" asked Jessame.

Grandpa tapped the side of his nose.

"It's a secret," he said. "Now go to sleep."

The whirring began again. And it whirred again the next night.

Jessame asked for a drink of water again and Grandpa brought her one.

"What *is* Mum making?" asked Jessame.

Grandpa tapped the side of his nose again.

"Please, Grandpa, give me a clue?"

Grandpa thought for a bit. Then he said,

"It's made by a worm
 But it won't make you squirm.
 It's made by your mum,
 It will cover your tum.
 It's made by night
 To give Jessame delight."

Then he kissed her and put out the light.

Jessame lay in the darkness thinking. "Made by a worm" was a bit worrying. All she could think of were the whirly worm casts on the grass in Victoria Park. She didn't want to wear something which looked like mud; that *would* make her squirm. What could it be?

The whirring went on, night after night, but at last the day of the Fancy Dress Party arrived. Surely now her mum would let her see? But no, at breakfast Mum said it wasn't quite ready yet. She would bring it to school in the afternoon.

"But what about your work?" said Jessame. "What about Mr Hankins at the Post Office? Who will write his letters?"

Mrs Olusanya said that as it was a very special day, Mr Hankins had said she could have a day's holiday, to finish the dress and take it to Jessame and see the Fancy Dress Parade.

Everyone else took their fancy dress costumes in the morning. Mrs Pearce said they were to put them in the cloakroom till after lunch, but she had to say it three times before everyone believed her. Jason said he ought to keep an eye on his beetle costume or it might scurry away into a dark corner and never be seen again. Jamila said someone might pick up her newspaper costume and take it away and read it, and the three McFigginses said their turtles might jump into the lavatories and swim into the sewers if they were left alone.

Mrs Pearce said everybody was being very silly – which Jessame thought was a bit unfair, because she wasn't being silly at all. Then Mrs Pearce said if everyone wasn't very sensible, there wouldn't be a Fancy Dress Party – and then there was a scramble for the cloakroom. Morning lessons followed but they went very, very slowly.

Jessame kept looking at the door, but Mrs Olusanya didn't come. She hadn't come by dinner time, and Jessame could hardly eat for worrying whether she would come, and wondering what her costume would be like when she did. Mrs Lal, the dinner-lady, said she must eat a little bit more or she would be poorly in the afternoon, so there was Jessame in the dinner hall, trying to eat cornflake crunch, and looking at the door. At last she saw her mum. She was holding a very big suitcase. But it wasn't till they were in the classroom that her mum opened the case – and there was the Very Fancy Dress.

Jessame couldn't say anything. She just hugged her mum very tightly round the middle. The dress looked exactly like the one in the museum, except that the blue material was an even prettier blue and it had a silver haze. It had the same nipped-in waist that ended in two points, the same little covered buttons, the same lace round the top of the bodice and the ruffles round the cuffs, and of course the same sticking-out skirt with *paniers*. And there was something else which looked a bit peculiar, a bit like a cage with sausage-shaped things on it.

Mum said it was a frame to make the sticking-out skirt stick out more. She helped Jessame to put it on, and then to put the Very Fancy Dress over it. There was hardly room to stand. Mum and Jessame had to move two tables, which was quite difficult because there were so many children standing there, gazing at the Very Fancy Dress. And then there were Grandma and Grandpa! Grandpa had his camera.

"Look like a lady, Jessame Aduke!"

Click!

"Curtsey, Jessame Aduke!"

Click!

Then Jessame showed Grandma and Grandpa the silver haze in the blue material and the ruffles round the cuffs and the ever so tiny waist, and she said, "Why did you say it was made by worms, Grandpa?"

"Because it's made of silk, real silk, made by silk worms."

That was amazing. Grandpa said they could read all about it later. Right now he wanted to know if the Very Fancy Dress was very uncomfortable.

"No," said Jessame, and she showed him the cage thing with the sausage shapes.

Grandpa thought they were very funny.

"They're to make your bottom stick out," he said, "and roll from side to side like a ship at sea. And do you know what they're called, Jessame Aduke? Do you know what their proper name is?"

"No."

"Bum rolls," said Grandpa.

"Quiet, Thomas," said Grandma Williams, looking all around to make sure no one had heard him. Then she gave Grandpa a very hard stare and Jessame couldn't stop laughing.

*illustrated by Caroline Sharpe*

The dress in this story is now on show at the Victoria and Albert Museum in London.

# THE PEDLAR OF SWAFFHAM

*East Anglian folk tale, retold by Kevin Crossley-Holland*

ONE night John Chapman* had a dream. A man stood by him, dressed in a surcoat as red as blood; and the man said, "Go to London Bridge. Go and be quick. Go, good will come of it."

John the pedlar woke with a start. "Cateryne," he whispered, "Cateryne, wake up! I've had a dream."

Cateryne, his wife, groaned and tossed and turned. "What?" she said.

"I've had a dream."

"Go to sleep, John," she said; and she fell asleep again.

John lay and wondered at his dream; and while he lay wondering he too fell asleep. But the man in scarlet came a second time, and said, "Go to London Bridge. Go and be quick. Go, good will come of it."

The pedlar sat up in the dark. "Cateryne!" he growled. "Wake up! Wake up! I've had the same dream again."

Cateryne groaned and tossed and turned. "What?" she said.

*You can find the meaning of these words at the end of the story.

Then John told her his dream.

"You," she said, "you would believe anything."

The moment he woke next morning, the pedlar of Swaffham remembered his dream. He told it to his children, Margaret and Hue and Dominic. He told it to his wife again.

"Forget it!" said Cateryne.

So John went about his business as usual and, as usual, his mastiff* went with him. He fed his pig and hens in the back yard. He hoisted his pack on his broad shoulders and went to the marketplace; he set up his stall of pots and pans, household goods of one kind and another, phials and potions, special trimmings for ladies' gowns. He gossiped with his friends – the butcher, the baker, the smith, the shoemaker and the weaver, the dyer and many another. But no matter what he did, the pedlar could not escape his dream. He shook his lion-head, he rubbed his blue eyes, but the dream seemed real and everything else seemed dreamlike. "What am I to do?" he said.

And his mastiff opened his jaws, and yawned. That evening John Chapman walked across the marketplace to the tumbledown church. And there he found the thin priest, Master Fuller; his holy cheekbones shone in the half-light. "Well, what is it?" Master Fuller said. Then John told him about his strange dream.

"I dream, you dream, everyone dreams," said the priest impatiently, swatting dust from his black gown. "Dream of how we can get gold to rebuild our church! This ramshackle place is an insult to God."

The two of them stood and stared sadly about them: all the walls of stone were rickety and uneven; the roof of the north aisle had fallen in, and through it they could see the crooked spire.

John Chapman gave a long sigh. "Gold," he said. "I wish I could."

Then the pedlar left the church and went back to his small cottage. But he was still uneasy. Nothing he did, and nothing anyone had said, seemed to make any difference; he could not forget his dream.

That night Cateryne said, "You've talked and talked of the man with the surcoat as red as blood. You've been more dreaming than awake. Perhaps, after all, you must go to London Bridge."

"I'll go," said John. "I'll go and be quick."

Next day, John Chapman got up at first light. At once he began to make ready for his journey. He hurried about, he banged his head against a beam, his face turned red. "I must take five gold pieces," he said, "I must take my cudgel."

"You must take your hood," said Cateryne.

Then John looked at his mastiff. "I must take you," he said. And the mastiff thumped the ground with his tail; dust and chaff flew through the air.

"Tell no one where I've gone," said John Chapman. "I don't want to be the laughing-stock of Swaffham."

Then, while the pedlar ate his fill of meat and curds, Cateryne put more food into his pack – cheese, and two loaves made of beans and bran, and a gourd* full of ale.

So everything was ready. And just as the June sun rose behind a light cloud, a great coin of gold, John kissed his wife and his children goodbye.

"Come back!" called little Dominic.

They stood by the door, the four of them, waving and waving until the pedlar with his pack, his cudgel and his mastiff, had walked out of Swaffham; out of sight.

John Chapman strode past the archery butts* just outside the town; he hurried between fields white with sheep. At first he knew the way well, but then the rough highway that men called the Gold Road* left the open fields behind and passed through sandy heathland where there were no people, no sheep, no villages.

Soon the rain came, heavy, blurring everything. John pulled his hood over his head, but the water seeped through it. It soaked through his clothes and dripped from his nose.

By midday, he was tired and steaming. So he stopped to eat food and give a bone to his mastiff. And while they ate, some lord's messenger, decked out in red and blue, galloped by and spattered them with mud.

"The devil take him!" the pedlar said.

During the afternoon, the rain eased and the pedlar and his dog were able to quicken their pace. One by one, the milestones dropped away; they made good progress.

But that evening it grew dark before the pedlar could find any shelter, even a peasant's shack or some deserted hovel. John had no choice but to sleep in the open, under an oak tree. "God help us," he said, "if there are wolves."

But there were no wolves, only strange nightsounds: the tree groaning and creaking, wind in the moaning leaves and the wind in the rustling grass, the barking of fox and vixen. When first light came, John could barely get to his feet for the ache in his cold bones and the cramp in his empty stomach.

And his mastiff hobbled about as if he were a hundred.

So for four days they walked. Each hour contained its own surprise; John talked to a friendly priest who had been to Jerusalem; he kept company with a couple of vagabonds who wanted him to go to a fair at Waltham; he shook off a rascally pardoner* who tried to sell him a ticket to heaven; he saw rabbits, and hares, and deer; he gazed down from hill-crests at tapestries of fields; he followed the way through dark forests where only silence lived. Never in his life had John seen so many strangers nor set eyes on so many strange things. "I'll tell you what," he said to his mastiff, "you and I are foreigners in our own country."

Sometimes the pedlar's pack chafed at his shoulders; often he envied the many travellers with horses – pilgrims and merchants, scholars and monks; but not for one moment did he forget his purpose. For as long as it was light, John Chapman made haste, following the Gold Road south towards London. And each night, after the first, he stayed at a wayside inn.

On the morning of the fifth day, the pedlar and his dog came at last to the City of London. At the sight of the high walls, John's heart quickened, and so did his step.

And his mastiff leaped about, barking for excitement.

They hurried through the great gate; and there before them were crowds of people coming and going, to-ing and fro-ing; men shouting their wares; women jostling and gossiping; small children begging; and many, many others sitting in rags in the filthy street. And there were houses to left and right; and after that, more houses, more streets, and always more people. John had never seen such a sight nor smelt such a stink nor heard such a hubbub.

A tide of people swept him along until he came to a place where four ways met. There, John stopped a man and asked him the way to London Bridge.

"Straight on," said the man. "Straight as an arrow's flight, all the way." The broad river gleamed under the sun, silver and green, ruckled by wind; gulls swooped and climbed again, shrieking. The great bridge spanned the water, the long bridge with its houses overhanging the river. It was a sight to gladden any man. And when he saw it, John Chapman got to his knees. He thanked God that his journey had been safe, and that he had come at last to London Bridge. But the moment the pedlar stepped on to the bridge itself he felt strangely foolish. All his hope and excitement seemed long ago. People were passing this way and that, but no one so much as looked at him. No one took the least notice of him. Having at last found London Bridge, the poor pedlar of Swaffham felt utterly lost.

He walked up and down; he stared about him; he watched

boats shoot the bridge; he added up his money. Hour after hour
after hour went by; the pedlar waited.

Late that afternoon, a group of pilgrims on horseback gathered
on the bridge. And they began to sing: *As you came from the holy-
land of Walsingham...*

"Walsingham!" cried John. "I know it well. I've taken my
wares there a hundred times. Will this song explain my dream?"

As if to answer him, the group of pilgrims broke up and rode
off, still singing, even as he hurried towards them.

"Wait!" bawled John. "Wait!"

But the hooves of the horses clattered and the poor pedlar was
left, in the fading light, looking after them. John felt heavy-
hearted. He wearily asked a passer-by where he might stay,
and was directed to The Three Cranes, a hostelry on the
riverbank, a stopping-place for passengers coming
down the river, a sleeping-place for
travellers in all weathers.

There John Chapman and his mastiff shared a bed of straw; they were both dog-tired.

Early on the morning of the second day the pedlar and his dog returned to the bridge. Once again, hour after hour went by. But late that day John saw a man with matted red hair lead a loping black bear across the bridge. "Look!" he exclaimed delightedly.

And his mastiff looked, carefully.

"A rare sight!" said John. "A sight worth travelling miles to see. Perhaps here I shall find the meaning of my dream." So the pedlar greeted the man; and he thought he had never seen anyone so ugly in all his life. "Does the bear dance?" he asked.

"He does," said the man. He squinted at John. "Give me gold and I'll show you."

"Another time," said the pedlar. And he stepped forward to pat the bear's gleaming fur.

"Hands off!" snapped the man.

"Why?" asked John.

"He'll have your hand off, that's why."

The pedlar stepped back hastily and called his mastiff to heel.

"He had a hand off at Cambridge," said the man.

"Not the best companion," said John.

"He'll bite your head off!" growled the man, and he squinted more fiercely than ever.

So the second day turned out no better than the first. And on the third day the poor pedlar waited and waited, he walked up and down and he walked to and fro, and no good came of it. "Now we have only one piece of gold left," he said to his mastiff. "Tomorrow we'll have to go home; I'm a great fool to have come at all."

At that moment a man shaped like an egg waddled up to John. "For three days," he said, "you've been loitering on this bridge."

"How do you know?" asked John, surprised.

"From my shop I've seen you come and go, come and go from dawn to dusk. What are you up to? Who are you waiting for?"

"That's exactly what I was asking myself," said the pedlar sadly. "To tell you the truth, I've walked to London Bridge because I dreamed that good would come of it."

"Lord preserve me!" exclaimed the shopkeeper. "What a waste of time!"

John Chapman shrugged his shoulders and sighed; he didn't know what to say.

"Only fools follow dreams," said the shopkeeper. "Why, last night I had a dream myself. I dreamed a pot of gold lay buried by a hawthorn tree in a garden; and the garden belonged to some pedlar, in a place called Swaffham."

"A pot of gold?" said John. "A pedlar?"

"You see?" said the egg-shaped man. "Nonsense!"

"Yes," said John.

"Dreams are just dreams," said the shopkeeper with a wave of his pudgy hand. "You're wasting your time. Take my advice and go back home."

"I will!" said John Chapman.

So it was that, in the evening of the twelfth day after his departure, John Chapman and his dog – spattered with mud, aching and blistered, weary but excited – returned home. They saw the leaning church spire; they passed the archery butts; they came at last to John's small cottage of wattle and daub.

Cateryne had never in her life been so glad to see her husband.

Margaret and Hue leaped about and their ashen hair danced on their heads.

"Come back!" cried little Dominic.

"So," asked Cateryne, "what of the dream, John?"

Then John told them in his own unhurried way. He told them of his journey; he told them of the long days on London Bridge; and, at last, he told them of the shopkeeper's words.

"A man follows one dream and returns with another," said Cateryne. "How can it all be true?"

"I've asked myself that a thousand times," the pedlar said, "and there's only one way to find out."

The gnarled hawthorn tree stood at the end of the yard; it had lived long, perhaps hundreds of years. And now its leaves seemed to whisper secrets.

The hens clucked in the dusk; and the pig lay still, one eye open, watching John.

"I'll start here," said the pedlar quietly. Then he gripped his round-edged spade and began to dig, making a mound of the loose earth.

"Can I?" asked Margaret.

"Let me!" said Hue.

"Wait!" said John. And again he dug. The spade bit into the packed soil.

At once they heard it, the grind of metal against metal, muted by soil. The pedlar took one look at his family and began to dig as fast as he could. Earth flew through the air. "Look!" he gasped. "Look! Look!" He had partly uncovered a great metal pot.

John tossed away his spade. He bent down and tugged. He
worked his fingers further under the pot and tugged again. Then
suddenly the dark earth gave up its secret. John staggered
backwards, grasping the pot and, as he fell, the lid flew off. The
ground was carpeted with gold!

At first they were all utterly silent. Only the tree, the tree in the
gloom went on whispering.

"Well! Gather it up," said the pedlar, slapping earth and straw
from his surcoat with his great hands. "Take it inside."

They picked up the gold coins and put them back into the pot.
Then they carried the pot into their cottage, and placed it on the
floor in front of the fire.

"Look! What's this?" said Hue, rubbing the lid of the pot. "It's
writing."

John frowned and shook his head. "It's words," he said. "I
know, I'll hide the gold here and take the empty pot with the rest
of my wares to the marketplace. Someone is sure to come along
and read it for us."

Next morning the pedlar was early in the marketplace, and
before long Master Fuller came picking his way towards him
through the higgledy-piggledy stalls – a dark figure amongst bright
colours, a silent man in a sea of noise.

"John Chapman," he exclaimed.
"Where have you been?"

"To and fro," said the pedlar.

"And where were you last Sunday?" asked the priest. "I missed
you at mass."

"Well, I…"

"Excuses! Always excuses!" said the priest sharply. "Who shall be saved? Men are empty vessels." And he rapped the great metal pot with his knuckles; it rang with a fine deep note. "Now that's a fine vessel!" said Master Fuller.

"It is," agreed John Chapman.

"There are words on it," said the priest. He raised the lid and narrowed his eyes. "It's in Latin. It says, *Under me… yes… Under me there lies another richer than I.*" The priest frowned. "What does that mean?"

John Chapman scratched the back of his head.

"Where did you get it?"

"Out of a back yard," said the pedlar, shrugging his broad shoulders.

"I must go," said the priest suddenly. "All this idle chatter. Men would do better to give time to God." And with that, the priest walked off towards the rickety church.

At once, the pedlar packed up his wares and hurried home.

"This time you shall dig," he told his children. Then Hue grasped the spade and began to dig; the rounded edge sheared through the darkness. His face soon flushed; he began to pant.

"Now let Margaret have it," the pedlar said.

Hue scowled, and handed the spade to his sister.

Margaret threw back her hair and stepped into the pit, and dug yet deeper. Deeper and deeper. Then, once again, metal grated against metal – the same unmistakable sound. Margaret shivered with excitement. "You," she said, and handed the spade back to her father.

Once more John dug as fast as he could; once more he tugged and tugged; and once more the reluctant earth yielded its secret – a second great pot, an enormous pot twice as large as the first. The pedlar could barely heave it out of the hole and on to the level ground. When he levered off the lid, they all saw that this pot too was heaped to the brim with glowing gold. "It's like a dream," said John, "and because of a dream. But we're awake, and rich."

Cateryne stared into the gaping, black hole. "Who hid it there?" she said. "And why?"

"Someone who lived here before us?" said the pedlar. "Or travellers on the Gold Road? How shall we ever know? People always say the hawthorn tree is a magic tree."

"What are we going to do with it?" asked Cateryne.

For a moment John did not reply. His blue eyes closed, his face wrinkled. "I know," he said at last. "I know. A little we'll keep – enough to pay for our own small needs, enough to buy ourselves a strip of land. But all the rest, every coin, we must give to Master Fuller to build the new church."

Cateryne drew in her breath and smiled and clapped her hands. "Amen!" she said.

"Amen!" chimed the children.

"In this way," said John, "everyone in Swaffham will share in the treasure."

"Now," said Cateryne, "and in time to come."

That afternoon, John Chapman found the priest skulking in the gloom of the tumbledown church. "Master Fuller," he said, "I can give gold for the new church."

"You?" said the priest. "Gold?"

"Wait here," said the pedlar. He hurried out of the church and back to his cottage. There, he counted one hundred pieces of gold for his own needs and the needs of his family, and hid them in the inner room, under the bed of straw.

Then the pedlar and his wife, and Margaret and Hue, followed by Dominic and their loyal mastiff, carried the two pots to Swaffham Church. As they crossed the marketplace, they shouted to their friends, "Come with us! Come to the church!"

So the butcher, the baker, the smith, the shoemaker, and the weaver, the dyer and many another left their work. In no time, a great procession, curious and chattering, were filing into the silent church.

In the nave, John and Cateryne turned one pot upside down. Then Margaret and Hue emptied the other. A great mound of coins glowed mysteriously in the half-light.

The townspeople gasped and Master Fuller's eyes gleamed. "Explain!" he said.

So John Chapman told them the whole story from beginning to end. And no storyteller, before or since, has ever had such an audience.

"There's enough gold here," said Master Fuller, "to rebuild the north aisle, and the steeple." Then he raised his right hand. "Let us pray," he said, "and after that... let us sing and dance the night away."

"Sing in the churchyard? Dance in the churchyard?" everyone cried.

"Even until this old church falls down," said Master Fuller. And for the first time that anyone could remember, he laughed. He threw back his head and laughed.

So, that same evening, a man with a bugle and a man with a humstrum* and a man with cymbals and clappers* played as if they meant to raise the roof off every house in Swaffham. The townsfolk sang and danced until midnight. And John the dreamer was tossed by the dancers into the air, higher and higher, towards the stars.

And his mastiff sat on his haunches, and laughed.

*illustrated by Pam Smy*

As you came from the holy-land
Of Walsingham,
Met you not with my true love
By the way as you came?

How should I know your true love,
That have met many a one
As I came from the holy-land,
That have come, that have gone?

She is neither white nor brown,
But as the heavens fair;
There is none hath a form so divine
On the earth, in the air.

Such a one did I meet (good sir)
With angel-like face;
Who like a queen did appear
In her gait, in her grace.

*Anonymous*

## GLOSSARY FOR THE PEDLAR OF SWAFFHAM

*archery butts*      a mark or target for archery practice. By law every male peasant had to possess a longbow and arrows and practise regularly at the butts.

*chapman*      a pedlar who travels about with goods for sale. People were often called by their professions: for instance, Butcher, Cooper, Taylor, Smith.

*clappers*      castanets.

*the Gold Road*      a road from Lynn, the major port in Norfolk, to London. It was so called because of the valuable exports and imports carried along it.

*gourd*      a drinking bottle made from the hollowed shell of the gourd fruit.

*humstrum*      a one-stringed roughly-made musical instrument.

*mastiff*      a powerful dog with a large head, drooping ears and hanging jowls.

*pardoner*      a man authorised by the Pope to forgive sins in return for money. Sometimes pardoners were rascals, and thieved from the poor.

# HOW THE ELEPHANT BECAME
## *Ted Hughes*

THE unhappiest of all the creatures was Bombo. Bombo didn't know what to become. At one time he thought he might make a fairly good horse. At another time he thought that perhaps he was meant to be a kind of bull. But it was no good. Not only the horses, but all the other creatures too, gathered to laugh at him when he tried to be a horse. And when he tried to be a bull, the bulls just walked away shaking their heads.

"Be yourself," they all said.

Bombo sighed. That's all he ever heard: "Be yourself. Be yourself." What was himself? That's what he wanted to know.

So most of the time he just stood, with sad eyes, letting the wind blow his ears this way and that, while the other creatures raced around him and above him, perfecting themselves.

"I'm just stupid," he said to himself. "Just stupid and slow and I shall never become anything."

That was his main trouble, he felt sure. He was much too slow and clumsy – and so big! None of the other creatures were anywhere near so big. He searched hard to find another creature as big as he was, but there was not one. This made him feel all the more silly and in the way.

But this was not all. He had great ears that flapped and hung, and a long, long nose. His nose was useful. He could pick things

up with it. But none of the other creatures had a nose anything like it. They all had small neat noses, and they laughed at his. In fact, with that, and his ears, and his long white sticking-out tusks, he was a sight.

As he stood, there was a sudden thunder of hooves. Bombo looked up in alarm.

"Aside, aside, aside!" roared a huge voice. "We're going down to drink."

Bombo managed to force his way backwards into a painful clump of thorn-bushes, just in time to let Buffalo charge past with all his family. Their long black bodies shone, their curved horns tossed, their tails screwed and curled, as they pounded down towards the water in a cloud of dust. The earth shook under them.

"There's no doubt," said Bombo, "who they are. If only I could be as sure of what I am as Buffalo is of what he is."

Then he pulled himself together.

"To be myself," he said aloud, "I shall have to do something that no other creature does. Lion roars and pounces, and Buffalo charges up and down bellowing. Each of these creatures does something that no other creature does. So. What shall I do?"

He thought hard for a minute.

Then he lay down, rolled over on to his back, and waved his four great legs in the air. After that he stood on his head and lifted his hind legs straight up as if he were going to sunburn the soles of his feet. From this position, he lowered himself back on to his four feet, stood up and looked round. The others should soon get to know me by that, he thought.

Nobody was in sight, so he waited until a pack of wolves appeared on the horizon. Then he began again. On to his back, his legs in the air, then on to his head, and his hind legs straight up.

"Phew!" he grunted, as he lowered himself. "I shall need some practice before I can keep this up for long."

When he stood up and looked round him this second time, he got a shock. All the animals were round him in a ring, rolling on their sides with laughter.

"Do it again! Oh, do it again!" they were crying, as they rolled and laughed. "Do it again. Oh, I shall die with laughter. Oh, my sides, my sides!"

Bombo stared at them in horror.

After a few minutes the laughter died down.

"Come on!" roared Lion. "Do it again and make us laugh. You look so silly when you do it."

But Bombo just stood. This was much worse than imitating some other animal. He had never made them laugh so much before.

He sat down and pretended to be inspecting one of his feet, as if he were alone. And, one by one, now that there was nothing to laugh at, the other animals walked away, still chuckling over what they had seen.

"Next show same time tomorrow!" shouted Fox, and they all burst out laughing again.

Bombo sat, playing with his foot, letting the tears trickle down his long nose.

Well, he'd had enough. He'd tried to be himself, and all the animals had laughed at him.

That night he waded out to a small island in the middle of the great river that ran through the forest. And there, from then on, Bombo lived alone, seen by nobody but the little birds and a few beetles.

One night, many years later, Parrot suddenly screamed and flew up into the air above the trees. All his feathers were singed. The forest was on fire.

Within a few minutes, the animals were running for their lives.
Jaguar, Wolf, Stag, Cow, Bear, Sheep, Cockerel, Mouse, Giraffe –
all were running side by side and jumping over each other to get
away from the flames. Behind them, the fire came through the
treetops like a terrific red wind.

"Oh dear! Oh dear! Our houses, our children!" cried the
animals.

Lion and Buffalo were running along with the rest.

"The fire will go as far as the forest goes, and the forest goes on
for ever," they cried, and ran with sparks falling into their hair.
On and on they ran, hour after hour, and all they could hear was
the thunder of the fire at their tails.

On into the middle of the next day, and still they were running.

At last they came to the wide, deep, swift river. They could go
no further. Behind them the fire boomed as it leapt from tree
to tree. Smoke lay so thickly over the forest and the river that
the sun could not be seen. The animals floundered in the

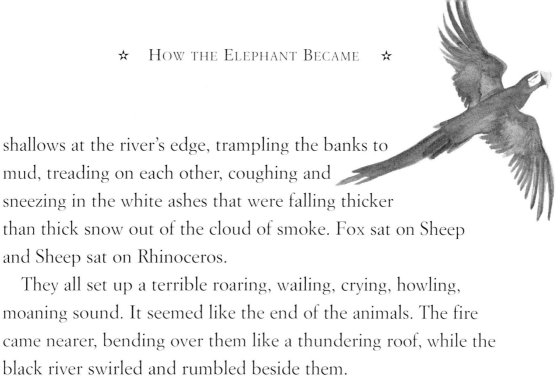

shallows at the river's edge, trampling the banks to
mud, treading on each other, coughing and
sneezing in the white ashes that were falling thicker
than thick snow out of the cloud of smoke. Fox sat on Sheep
and Sheep sat on Rhinoceros.

They all set up a terrible roaring, wailing, crying, howling,
moaning sound. It seemed like the end of the animals. The fire
came nearer, bending over them like a thundering roof, while the
black river swirled and rumbled beside them.

Out on his island stood Bombo, admiring the fire which made
a fine sight through the smoke with its high spikes of red flame.
He knew he was quite safe on his island. The fire couldn't cross
that great stretch of water very easily.

At first he didn't see the animals crowding low by the edge of
the water. The smoke and ash were too thick in the air. But soon
he heard them. He recognised Lion's voice shouting:

"Keep ducking yourselves in the water. Keep your fur wet
and the sparks will not burn you."

And the voice of Sheep crying:

"If we duck ourselves we're swept away by the river."

And the other creatures – Gnu, Ferret, Cobra, Partridge, crying:

"We must drown or burn. Goodbye, brothers and sisters!"

It certainly did seem like the end of the animals.

Without a pause, Bombo pushed his way into the water. The river was deep, the current heavy and fierce, but Bombo's legs were both long and strong. Burnt trees, that had fallen into the river higher up and were drifting down, banged against him, but he hardly felt them.

In a few minutes he was coming up into shallow water towards the animals. He was almost too late. The flames were forcing them, step by step, into the river, where the current was snatching them away.

Lion was sitting on Buffalo, Wolf was sitting on Lion, Wildcat on Wolf, Badger on Wildcat, Cockerel on Badger, Rat on Cockerel, Weasel on Rat, Lizard on Weasel, Tree-Creeper on Lizard, Harvest Mouse on Tree-Creeper, Beetle on Harvest Mouse, Wasp on Beetle, and on top of Wasp, Ant, gazing at the raging flames through his spectacles and covering his ears from their roar.

When the animals saw Bombo looming through the smoke, a great shout went up:

"It's Bombo! It's Bombo!"

All the animals took up the cry:

"Bombo! Bombo!"

Bombo kept coming closer. As he came, he sucked up water in his long, silly nose and squirted it over his back, to protect himself from the heat and the sparks. Then, with the same long, silly nose he reached out and began to pick up the animals, one by one, and seat them on his back.

"Take us!" cried Mole.

"Take us!" cried Monkey.

He loaded his back with the creatures that had hooves and big feet; then he told the little clinging things to cling on to the great folds of his ears. Soon he had every single creature aboard. Then he turned and began to wade back across the river, carrying all the animals of the forest towards safety.

Once they were safe on the island they danced for joy. Then they sat down to watch the fire. Suddenly Mouse gave a shout:

"Look! The wind is bringing sparks across the river. The sparks are blowing into the island trees. We shall burn here too."

As he spoke, one of the trees on the edge of the island crackled into flames. The animals set up a great cry and began to run in all directions.

"Help! Help! Help! We shall burn here too!"

But Bombo was ready. He put those long, silly tusks of his, that he had once been so ashamed of, under the roots of the burning tree and heaved it into the river. He threw every tree into the river till the island was bare. The sparks now fell on to the bare, torn ground, where the animals trod them out easily. Bombo had saved them again.

Next morning the fire had died out at the river's edge.

The animals on the island looked across at the smoking, blackened plain where the forest had been. Then they looked round for Bombo.

He was nowhere to be seen.

"Bombo!" they shouted. "Bombo!" And listened to the echo.

But he had gone. He is still very hard to find. Though he is huge and strong, he is very quiet.

But what did become of him in the end? Where is he now?

Ask any of the animals, and they will tell you:

"Though he is shy, he is the strongest, the cleverest, and the kindest of all the animals. He can carry anything and he can push anything down. He can pick you up in his nose and wave you in the air. We would make him our king if we could get him to wear a crown."

*illustrated by Jackie Morris*

# ACKNOWLEDGEMENTS

*We would like to thank the following authors, publishers and agents for their kind permission to reproduce copyright material.*

**The Emperor's New Clothes** from *Hans Christian Andersen's Fairy Tales* translated by Naomi Lewis (Puffin, 1981) © Naomi Lewis, 1981. **Beauty and the Beast** from *Beauty and the Beast and Other Stories* retold by Adèle Geras (Hamish Hamilton, 1996) © Adèle Geras, 1996. **The Riddle-Me-Ree** by Alison Uttley from *The Adventures of Tim Rabbit* published by Faber and Faber Ltd. **The Beast With a Thousand Teeth** by Terry Jones reprinted by permission of Pavilion Books from *Fairy Tales* by Terry Jones. **A Necklace of Raindrops** by Joan Aiken from *A Necklace of Raindrops* by Joan Aiken published by Jonathan Cape. **The Disastrous Dog** by Penelope Lively from *Uninvited Ghosts* published by Heinemann Young Books Limited (a division of Egmont Children's Books Limited). **Clever Cakes** by Michael Rosen 'Clever Cakes' from *Clever Cakes and Other Stories* Text © 1991 Michael Rosen. Illustrated by Caroline Holden. Reproduced by permission of the publisher Walker Books Ltd., London. **A Lullaby for Freddy** by Adèle Geras © Adele Geras 1991. Permission granted by the author. **Runaway** from *Lion at School and Other Stories* by Philippa Pearce (Viking/Kestrel, 1985) © Philippa Pearce, 1971. **The Heartless Giant** from *Jim Henson's The Storyteller*, folk tales retold by Anthony Minghella (Alfred A. Knopf, Inc.) © 1991 The Jim Henson Company. All Rights Reserved. **The Boy With Two Shadows** by Margaret Mahy from *A Lion in the Meadows* © Margaret Mahy published by Orion Children's Books. **The Girl and the Crocodile** by Leila Berg from *Tales for Telling* published by Heinemann Young Books (a division of Egmont Children's Books Limited). **Teddy Robinson's Night Out** by Joan Robinson from *About Teddy Robinson* by Joan G Robinson (Puffin Books, 1974) © Joan G Robinson, 1959. **A Drink of Water** by John Yeoman by permission of A.P Watt Ltd. on behalf of John Yeoman. **The Little Girl and The Tiny Doll** by Aingelda Ardizzone from *Time for a Tale* edited by Julia Eccleshare. Reproduced by permission of Hodder and Stoughton Limited. **Tomkin and the Three Legged Stool** by Vivian French 'Tomkin and the Three Legged Stool' from *The Thistle Princess and Other Stories* Text © 1995 Vivian French. Illustrated by Chris Fisher. **The Mossy Rock** from *A Book of Sorcerers and Spells*, folk tales retold by Ruth Manning-Sanders, published by Methuen. Reproduced by permission of David Higham Associates Ltd. **The Kingdom Under The Sea** from *The Orchard Book of Magical Tales* retold by Margaret Mayo, (Orchard Books, 1993) © Margaret Mayo, 1993. **Jessame and the Very Fancy Dress** by Julia Jarman from *Jessame Stories*, published by Heinemann Young Books (a division of Egmont Children's Books Limited). **The Pedlar of Swaffham** from *The Old Stories, Folk Tales from East Anglia and The Fen Country* retold by Kevin Crossley-Holland (Colt Books, 1997) © Kevin Crossley-Holland 1997. **How the Elephant Became** by Ted Hughes from *How the Whale Became* published by Faber and Faber Ltd.

Every effort has been made to obtain permission from all copyright holders whose material is included in this book, but in some cases this has not proved possible. We wish to thank those authors who are included without acknowledgement. Faber and Faber apologize for any errors or omissions in the above list and would be grateful to be notified of any corrections that should be incorporated in the next edition of this volume.